To, —

Not to us
but to
them be all
the glory

No Hands But Yours

Love

A Chronicle of God's Love, Through His Servants, After the Haitian Earthquake

April

By April Perry

James 2:5

All proceeds from the sales of this book will go directly to help the work in Haiti through Luke's Mission, Inc.

Luke's Mission is a Christian nonprofit organization that works in Haiti supporting education for health care providers and advancing public health projects both in urban and rural settings.

Contributions are tax deductible and can be sent to:

Luke's Mission, Inc
1403 Mason Road
Durham, NC 27712

"Christ has no body now on earth but yours,
No hands but yours
No feet on earth but yours.

Yours are the feet with which
He walks to do good.

Yours are the hands with which
He blesses all the world.

Yours are the hands, yours are the feet,
Yours are the eyes, you are His body.

Yours are the eyes with which
He looks compassion on this world.

Christ has no body now on earth but yours"

St. Teresa of Avila
(1515-1582)
Public Domain

Jesus, with us abide.
Abide with us, that so this life
Of suffering over past,
An Easter of unending joy
We may attain at last.

Claudia F. Hernaman,
Child's Book of Praise; A Manual of Devotion in Simple Verse,
1873
Public Domain

*Therefore we will not fear,
though the earth give way and
the mountains fall into the
heart of the sea.*

Psalms 46:2

Table of Contents

Acknowledgements

My sincerest gratitude to the following people who helped with the publication of this book:

Eddy-my translator and beloved friend
Carol Ann Mullis and my mom Joyce Perry for their editorial skills
Ben Lichius for his design of the cover
Members and friends at Aldersgate UMC for their support during the earthquake and the times afterwards
Judy Darnell, Bronwyn Bartle, Karen Hassell and Carol Meguid for their special and memorable words of encouragement
Shelia Rittgers- my best friend and co-worker in Haiti
NC Baptist men for allowing me to travel with their group
All of the missionaries at Global Outreach Haiti without whom we could not have done our work
Starr Browning for her support of my Haiti work
The Duke MLK Selection committee for their generous gift to our work
Emmanuel for being our hands and feet in Haiti and doing work on the ground for us after the earthquake

Introduction

December 1, 2010

The vast majority of this book was written within the first 3 weeks of my return. From the moment I knew I was going to be able to travel to Haiti after the earthquake, I had a strong compulsion that part of my purpose in this whole thing was to help to bring the story of what happened in Haiti back to the people here.

I have often found words completely inadequate to describe the things I have seen in Haiti. That being said, my first book seemed to make the points that I wanted with words alone so I felt if I could get my thoughts on paper quickly, they would be more effective in expressing the story of post earthquake Haiti.

What I didn't anticipate was the reaction I would have once things began to settle in several weeks after my return. I worked diligently doing what we needed for Luke's Mission and with the Lord's strength we accomplished many things for a small organization. In retrospect, I see that I was really using my energy as a distraction-a valuable one- but a distraction none the less, from what I had encountered in post-earthquake Haiti. That was nearly a full time job but along with my "day job" it provided little time for me to reflect on what I had just experienced.

My plan was to have this book out within three months of my experience. The story was fresh, people were more than interested and the typical short news cycle of this story didn't seem to be playing itself out like it had with other disasters. So as long as the story was interesting, I wanted to capitalize on that for the sake of the Haitian people.

However, it was 8 months before I could bring myself to get back to this book. A friend described my experience as "having things stored in my hard drive. They just weren't ready to print yet". Each time I thought I should work on finishing it, I just couldn't bring myself to do it.

I was reassured by those who know these things-i.e. the professionals-that this kind of response is not only perfectly normal but expected when one has encountered the kinds of horrific scenes that I encountered while in Haiti. The fact that my training kicked in and that I was able to function in a way that provided me with a sense of being able to help was to be a mark of the inner strength the Lord had given me in this situation.

One doesn't walk away from seeing mass graves, immeasurable suffering, hundreds of dead and dying, children loosing legs, arms or both, head injuries, spinal cord injuries, starvation and disease and not remained unchanged and affected.

Not everyone could have or should have gone. But my job was to go. Yours may be to read these words and respond in the way the Lord puts on your heart.

The time has come for this book as the first anniversary of the earthquake is approaching. My hope is that as people read these pages, they will again consider what their part is in the cause and solution of the problem that the Haitian earthquake has now presented us with—us meaning the collective body humanity of because it is all of us who now need to respond to it.

NOTE: Exact text is used for text messages and emails that are reproduced in this book. Grammatical and spelling errors in those sections are intentional.

Chapter 1
<u>No hands but yours...</u>

"I'm afraid we might know some people who are dead now."

Hearing those words is how January 13, 2010 started for me. After I got up, I came down early to get my coffee and check my email. Shelia is my long time best friend and is closer than a sister to me and my family. She lives with me and serves with me as the vice chairman of Luke's Mission. She was sitting at the table with tears in her eyes.

Usually I am the one who displays the overt emotions related to most events that we encounter together. But this time, it was Shelia—the one who often gathers all the information and then carefully formulates a response to it. She was clearly scared that we knew people who might now be dead following the massive 7.0 earthquake of January 12, 2010 in Haiti.

The reality is that the events of that time period actually started months before for me. So many things would weave themselves together like a finely made tapestry to bring me to the place I would find myself that morning.

4 months earlier
The first threads of that tapestry came together in early October, 2009. I got an email from a colleague who wanted to coordinate a nomination for me for the annual Martin Luther King Community Caregiver Award. This is an award given by Duke University Health System as part of their annual commemoration events for MLK day. The award honors the volunteer efforts of

4

those employees who work outside of their "day jobs" to improve life for those around them.

Initially I was skeptical that I would even qualify. I wasn't sure that my international work in Haiti would meet the criteria. The award seemed to be more focused on inspiring people to volunteer in the community by honoring someone who did that. But as I read the nomination criteria and their definition of community- "Community will be defined as local, national and international arenas"-I thought what the heck? Wouldn't it be great to get that kind of money for the people of Haiti? Even then the focus for me was not on the award and what it might say about me but more about how we might use the money to further our work.

Awards of this kind are rare at Duke. Duke is the largest employer in the city of Durham—employing about 25,000 people. While the quality of medical care given at Duke is first rate and unsurpassed elsewhere, its very size prevents it from being a cozy "mom and pop" place of employment. It is hard to do things for all of those employees that are really meaningful like you can do in much smaller places of employment. I joked with a colleague that usually we get something like a Starbuck's gift card as a way of acknowledging something special that we had done. So to have an award which not only acknowledged the contribution of the honoree but had some backbone behind it in the amount of a monetary award of $5000 to the organization that the award winner served with made it very appealing.

My colleague, Carol Ann, asked me to assist her in preparing the nomination by providing her with some information. She wanted names of some people who might agree to write a letter of nomination. I supplied those for her and an outline of the work that I did including some situations which might make the case for how Luke's Mission was improving people's lives in Haiti over the last 8 years.

As the months went by, periodically she would send me the nomination letters-there would be 21 in all-from those people whose names I had supplied to her. She emailed the people who I had suggested and in turn, most emailed her back their part of the submission. Each time I read one, I was moved as they described my work in Haiti from their perspective. Some had traveled to Haiti with me. Their perspectives were profound. Others had seen what I had done here as I tried to work for the people of Haiti here-raising money, giving talks, bringing the troubling story of Haiti to interested people here in the US.

Two situations were central to the nomination. The first one was the story of a translator, Romel Dorsaint, whom I had met on my first trip to Haiti. He had shown such promise and wanted so much to become a doctor. But coming from Cite Soleil, the poorest slum in North and South America, the chances of that happening were virtually nil. However, my heart was moved by him and I came home determined to do all I could to try to help him achieve his dream.

I guess it was good that I didn't really think about what I was getting myself into. The thought of what it might take to raise nearly $50,000 over the next 7 years would have been paralyzing frightening to me and I likely wouldn't have gone forward. I realized later that God protected me from myself with a layer of denial, or idealism, whichever one you want to call it, at that point in time that allowed me to be obedient to Him and move forward with this plan. Clearly, it was a plan which was ordained by Him. More threads in the tapestry.

In 2002, I founded Luke's Mission, a registered 501C3 nonprofit, as a means to allow people to donate money to help Romel and eventually others who wanted to provide health care in Haiti to help care for their people. As time went on we expanded our interests to promoting public health initiatives such as sanitation and hygiene projects, and clean water projects involving household water filtration systems.

3

But for Romel, it was a long 7 years of school. Beginning higher education brought with it challenges he had not faced in the past. Learning a new way of studying under the direst circumstances- no electricity, needing to go to the public park late at night just to be able to see his text books, lack of computer access- made his student life challenging and difficult.

In Romel's third year of medical school, the country underwent a coup d'état. Rebels from the northern region of the country grew unhappy with the current president, Jean-Bertrand Aristide, and began to take over the country from the north. As they progressed south to the capital, tensions mounted. They wanted Aristide to leave the country and threatened to overthrow him, violently if needed. As they grew closer to the capital city, the pressure and threats mounted. People were afraid of a bloody confrontation that would end in many deaths.

Fortunately, with a great deal of international pressure, Aristide did flee the country in the middle of the night and went to South Africa where he remains to this day. But what followed afterwards was a UN peacekeeping occupation which continues today. As I write this in 2010, a great deal of instability, gang violence, further economic decline and loss of any integrity to the government continues. During this time, Romel's school operated sporadically but they did manage to stay within their time frame. By going one continuous year with no breaks, his was able to keep on the schedule that they started with.

In his sixth year, he made the difficult decision to get married. It wasn't difficult because of the woman he was to marry. Fregga and he had dated for over 10 years. But marrying prior to finishing school for both of them would add additional challenges and difficulties to their life. Fregga was also in school studying to be a nurse. Moving in together and away from their families would increase their stress while completing their studies.

4

Romel struggled with his grades the first few years. Education in Haiti is all based upon rote and very little conceptual teaching takes place. With few textbooks available in Haiti, I often had to order textbooks in French from an online book ordering service and get them to him. However, once he started his clinical rotations, he excelled. It was clear that he had a solid ability to put into practice with patients the knowledge that he was learning from books.

As the fall of 2009 progressed, Romel neared the end of his formal education. He was to graduate in November, 2009 and then complete a yearlong residency with a governmental hospital to earn his license to practice medicine. I was privileged to share in that day in his graduation and see him accept his diploma. It was a day that still hasn't fully registered with me. To think that I had a part in seeing this young man from the poorest slum in North and South America achieve his dream of becoming a physician is still surreal to me.

That was 6 weeks before the earthquake.

More colors being woven into that tapestry.

This was to be one of the first times that I was to know my hands were being used by the Master to further His work in Haiti.

The next story that was central to the nomination was one which had happened in June, 2008. I was leading our annual church mission trip to Haiti. We were working in Cahesse, Haiti a small village in the northern part of the country near Cap Haitian. We had a team of eight, with me and a hematologist/oncologist working as health care providers seeing patients and other team members providing support roles in the pharmacy, triage, and on the eye team.

My colleague and good friend Hank Van Deventer, the physician, walked into my room one afternoon. He clearly looked stunned.

He said to me, "I need your help with this woman. I have no idea what to do."

I had worked with Hank on several other trips. He is an accomplished and extremely compassionate physician. I have recommended him to a number of people, and if I had cancer, he is the first person I would seek out to care for me. His patients are very fortunate to have someone who is so knowledgeable, and has the caring heart that goes with his intellect, to provide the best care for them. I have found him to be extremely useful in Haiti. He tends to want to over think a lot of things in Haiti-out of his strong desire to do the best he can for any particular patient. He does it less now but this was several years before this writing. However, our care is so limited in Haiti it is often something that is difficult to come to grips with. Hank would be a regular in my room, reviewing cases with me making sure there wasn't something else we should be doing for a patient he was seeing.

I have to admit when Hank came into my room I expected it to be something rather routine for me in Haiti. I thought that he just needed reassurance for that he was doing the right thing and there was nothing further he could offer.

When I followed him into his exam room in the clinic we were working in, even I was surprised. There sat a Haitian woman with a bandana over the left side of her head covering the side of her face and neck. Her name was Madame Georges. As we removed the bandana, I saw a huge mass which about the size of a soccer ball. It had completely deformed her neck and face. The outer surface of it was necrotic-a medical term for rotting, dead tissue and it was infected. It was covered with flies and had a strong odor to it.

I didn't have to think about what we could do for her. From my extensive experience in providing medical care in Haiti, it was clear to me immediately that we couldn't help her. Additionally, from my knowledge of the Haitian medical care system (which is described later in this book), I knew she would not be able to find help there either. Hank and I examined her carefully, looking at and feeling the tumor to see how extensive it was, if it was connected to the bone underneath and if it was compressing her windpipe. Compression on the windpipe would be a serious acute problem we would need to deal with immediately. Thankfully, the tumor was not compressing the windpipe.

We discerned with her together through our translator that she had had this tumor for 8 years. She was still able to eat, swallow and breathe alright, although she had to make adjustments in how she ate. Both of us felt that it was unlikely a serious cancer because if it was, and she had indeed had it for eight years, it would very likely have spread to other organs by now and she would have succumbed to it long ago. Our best guess was that it was a common tumor of the salivary glands, a parotid tumor. The vast majority of these are benign. In the United States, these would be removed long before they got to this stage with few, if any, complications or secondary conditions.

I asked Hank to step out of the room and we talked about what to do. Obviously there was nothing we could do in our clinic to assist her. The problem I was most concerned about was the stigmatization that she had from the community because of this obnoxious tumor. She already had to hide herself from others and it was clear that she wouldn't be able to do any sort of work or employment with this tumor.

From my experience, I felt that sending her to the local Haitian hospital would be a waste of time and money. But something in me just felt like we should get a bit more information and pray about what to do.

Hank and I went into the room to talk to her. We decided to do what I have to do often in Haiti. We explained to Mme. Georges that we are not equipped to help her. She needed extensive surgery and I just wasn't sure that was available in Haiti. We offered her some pain medication but she wasn't in real pain. We offered to pray with her and she accepted. Finally, I noted her name and after she left, I asked one of the mission compound people if they knew her and where she lived. They said yes.

That evening, we all discussed this terrible situation in our devotion time. All of us felt terrible and deeply concerned about the quality of life of this woman and what her future would hold. We found out that she had four children at home she was trying to support and raise. I tucked all of this away in my mind for further thought, prayer and discernment.

When we left to return home, Shelia and I decided that we might want to investigate a couple of mission hospitals that we knew had a few more resources than the average Haitian hospital. We both felt that the skill level required to remove this complex tumor would be beyond any Haitian physician. Additionally, sophisticated anesthetic techniques were required and that is something that isn't available in Haiti on a daily basis.

We contacted two missionary run hospitals, one in Les Cayes Haiti and one in Northern Haiti. After several emails over a few days with both of them, the doctors there felt they just didn't have the equipment or personnel to deal with this problem.

I made contact with a mission hospital that is run from an organization in Charlotte, NC. They indicated an American surgeon, Bill TenHaaf, was going to be in Haiti in a few weeks and gave me his contact information. I emailed a picture of her that we had taken and asked him if he thought he might be able to see her when he was in Haiti for an evaluation. His response was this:

April:
I saw the picture, but, as you can imagine, it is hard
to see the extent of the tumor on a picture.
Palpation will tell me much more, I hope. I arrive
in Cayes on the 7th of August, whenever the first
flight out to Cayes from Port arrives (a real
question these days), so will see what we find out.
Bill

It was now August, 2008. We decided to pay one of our translators to take Mme. Georges to a missionary run hospital for them to at least see her and make any suggestions. Luminere Hospital is located on the southern peninsula of Haiti. I know some of the missionary doctors there and hoped that if they couldn't help her, they might be able to suggest someone who would. Our translator and assistant Emmanuel Occidor accompanied Mme. Georges to the hospital. She came down from the Cap Haitian area to Port au Prince. It is a seven hour bus ride, although it is only about 60 miles in distance. Emmanuel's family graciously allowed her and her son to stay with them for the night prior to making the rest of the trip the next day.

They took the four hour bus ride to Bonne Fin the following day and were to meet with the physicians in the afternoon for the appointment. However, as things often go in Haiti, "something" prevented the physicians from seeing patients that day. They had to quickly find a place to stay overnight and obtain food for the small group and wait until the next day.

Romel, our medical student, was doing a rotation at Luminere. He met Mme Georges and Emmanuel and took them to the clinic area. After a wait of a few hours, a physician finally saw her.

Now all of this sounds relatively easy, and is taking up very few lines in this book. But believe me, it wasn't easy. It required multiple emails over about 10 days, several phone calls, multiple trips to Western Union to send the money required for transportation, food and other logistics on the trip, cell phone calls back to us to report progress and a lot of prayers. And in the mean time Hurricanes Faye and Gustav hit Haiti killing hundreds there.

Her appointment was scheduled for August 8th. It was a long convoluted process-something which happens every moment of every day in Haiti.

Finally, we received the news in an email that I sent to the team members on August 11, 2008.

Please continue to pray for Mme Georges as we try to network to get her some help for this very large salivary gland tumor.

We spoke with Emmanuel at greater length this weekend. Dr. TenHaaf from the US saw her and could do the surgery but the ability to do general anesthesia at the mission hospital now doesn't exist. Broken equipment, no anesthesiologists or some other problems. Again nothing in Haiti is easy or uncomplicated. He returns to the US early next week and I can talk to him myself then.

So he referred her to a Haitian ENT doc nearby. The Haitian doc did not feel he could do this level of surgery. He did know of an American surgeon who might be able to help in Port au Prince. So Emmanuel and Mme. Georges returned to PAP on Saturday to go to the Hospital there to see him, Dr. Lazarre.

Unfortunately Dr. Lazarre is on vacation in the US for two weeks.

So we are again in the waiting game for him to return.
Emmanuel has letters/consultations from both of
the physicians who saw her and hopefully when Dr.
Lazarre returns he will set up an appt for her to see him
in the next few weeks.

In the mean time, I am going to network with a couple
other hospitals where I have contacts, Albert
Schweitzer Hospital and Partners in Health-Paul
Farmers hospital-to see if they can possibly help. I
met Paul Farmer a couple of years ago when we
were speaking at the same conference (a story in
itself-but the short version is I was in the unenviable
position of speaking immediately after him. We both
laughed about it before hand but I wasn't laughing after
hearing him and then stepping up to the podium.
Fortunately my topic-Voodoo and cultural health
care in Haiti-was interesting enough to make up for
the position I was in).

So please continue to pray for us as we try to get
this woman some help who is suffering immeasurably. I
prayed last night for wisdom and guidance from the
Holy Spirit on this matter. I would appreciate your
prayers for the same.
April

The bottom line was that the physician just didn't feel that they could undertake the operation without the appropriate infrastructure in place to make sure the patient had all of the benefits of a safe surgery. None of the physicians he referred us to did either. So we were back to square one.

I expressed my frustration and fatigue in an email to Hank later that evening:
August 9, 2008
Hank:

Note below for the truth from the on the ground American doc who is trying to help us. [He had described in the email a situation where no Haitian physicians at his clinic had received their licenses to practice from the government despite "graduating" 7 years previous which impacted his reluctance to take on this complicated case.]

So when people say they have a "nurse" or a "nurse practitioner" or even a doctor at their clinic, we need to be sure we understand the skills of these people and "ask the right questions" before we come to conclusions about their capabilities. Reading this I am overwhelmed with the need and can't think about it any longer today. Let's talk about this soon.
April

It had been a long and arduous six weeks of nearly constant efforts during my free waking hours to get to this point, only to find that all of our efforts had been futile. I had made some preliminary inquiries at Albert Schweitzer Hospital in De Chapalles, our last resort and had heard nothing back.

That was August 9, 2008.

I wrote to Emmanuel and told him we needed to step back and see what else, if anything, we could do but I didn't really have anything in mind. I was saddened but felt we had exhausted our efforts.

Then on August 12, three days later, I got an email from someone I rarely communicated with. She attended my church. I had been asking for prayer for Mme. Georges in the church service, explaining briefly that we were trying to find medical care for her. This woman wrote to me in an email that she had a friend that was in Haiti with her husband and she was writing a

blog.   She knew I worked in Haiti and thoug₁
interested in reading the blog.

I am always interested in other people's impressions c
began to read it.   It was lengthy but she describe╮   ₋y
eloquent terms what she was seeing and her responses ω them.
Something seemed to ring a bell with me.   I went back and
looked at her name—Meg McCann.   She mentioned her husband
worked at Duke and was in Haiti doing a 6 month sabbatical
there at Albert Schweitzer Hospital.   Things began to click in a
hurry.

McCann. …Physician at Duke….

I knew a Richard (Dick) McCann who was a renowned vascular
surgeon who had worked at Duke for over 40 years. Surely, this
couldn't be him? It was just too good to be true! I quickly wrote
my acquaintance back who had forwarded the blog to me and
asked her if this Meg McCann was Dr. Dick McCann's wife. I
waited with baited breath that afternoon for her answer. When it
came, I knew it was from the hand of the Lord.

Yes, Meg was Dick's wife. They had just arrived in Haiti about
one month before and Theo, the woman who sent me the blog,
was good friends with Meg. She just thought I might like to read
her blog. Never in a million years could she have known the
critical link her email would make in connecting me with the
person who could help Mme. Georges.

On August 14, I quickly emailed Dick at his Duke email account
which I had access to.

"Dick

> *Let me introduce myself. I am April Perry,*
> *currently an APRN who works at Duke HomeCare &*
> *Hospice but worked for years as a physician*
> *extender in various clinical areas at DUMC. I have*

13

been doing medical mission work in Haiti for the last 8 years, taking medical teams to the Port au Prince, Mirebalais and Cap Haitian areas and working with our non profit to promote public health initiatives in Haiti in a small village called Belbede right near HAS.

On our July trip this year I saw a 38 year old woman with a very large parotid mass which had been growing for eight years. The mass was now necrosing and fungating. She could breathe and swallow adequately but as you can imagine is suffering immeasurably. The mass is malodorous and infection is a serious concern. I am sure with a skilled surgeon this large mass could be removed even if it wasn't possible to do a nerve sparing procedure. Clearly if the mass continues to grow, it will ultimately cause her demise.

I am very familiar with the Haitian medical system and know there are no Haitian surgeons skilled enough to perform this procedure. I have looked into two American run mission hospitals but their infrastructure   will not support this surgery. Our church is committed to paying for the care of this woman if we can arrange for a skilled surgeon to do her surgery.

I do have some contacts at HAS and did make an inquiry of them last week but didn't hear anything back yet. However, I do know Theo Roddy, a friend of yours. She   goes to my church and heard me describe my desire for   our church to pray for us to try to find some help in Haiti for this woman.

When she informed me you were there, I wondered if it would be possible for you to at least evaluate her and see if you could perform the needed

14

parotidectomy for her. We do have an employee on the ground in Haiti who can bring you her medical records and accompany her to the visit, will make arrangements for her to stay for the surgery and her post operative care.

I am certain you could perform this surgery if HAS had adequate infrastructure to support general anesthesia-which she will require. What a god send it would be if we could work out for her to at least see you. If this is a possibility, please respond to me at this email and we will make arrangements for her and our employee to come to HAS for a consultation.

I am grateful for all you are doing now for my   beloved Haitian people and hope that all is going well as Meg indicated in her recent email Theo forwarded to me.

I will wait to hear from you.

April"

I waited to hear from him knowing that we were far from out of the woods. I received a reply back on August 18.

April:
I can see her in the HAS surgical clinic. We see elective cases M-W-F. We can do simple parotid surgery but if   the mass is fixed and invading the mandible it may be out of bounds.... There is a cost here 4,500 Haitian gourdes[about $562 US] for in-district citizens and twice for out. I don't know if she is in or out.

Richard

I could see the hand of the Lord, weaving this very intricate tapestry together to come up with a lovely picture. I didn't know if Dick could help Mme. Georges, but I knew he was skilled enough to do it and if he couldn't do it, I would have felt like we had done all we could.

I wrote to Emmanuel and asked him to go to Hopital Albert Schweitzer (HAS) and to take her records and pictures before we sent for her to make sure that Dr. McCann could indeed see her. Emmanuel took the bus there and set up a consultation appointment for August 27.

He evaluated it and believed it to be operable. She was scheduled to come back for some blood work and to bring two of her relatives to donate blood for her. He wanted to have eight units of matching blood on hand available for her before the surgery. So some of her relatives had to come to see if they matched and donate the blood. If their blood was a match, the surgery would be performed on Monday, October 6th.

She was scheduled for the surgery on that Monday.

It had been a long haul - three hospitals, four doctors and four hurricanes later- we were now able to procure the medical consult for her. He did think he could remove the tumor but needed for her to have 8 units of blood in reserve for the surgery. Emmanuel, our able interpreter, who had overseen this and had been with her through this whole process.

It is hard for many to understand what an undertaking it had been to get this woman some help. I hope you can see how the Lord has intervened because with our own strength and resources, it wouldn't have happened.

We asked everyone to pray for Mme Georges and her surgery. The night before the surgery Emmanuel called us and asked specifically that we ask the whole church to pray for him, Mme

Georges and her family during this process. Things looked like they might come together to relieve this woman's tremendous suffering but we weren't there yet.

Just to give you some perspective, the surgery was planned to cost about $700. This woman has been suffering immeasurably for lack of $700 to pay for surgery on this huge tumor. We anticipated some additional expenses related to her post-operative care. It is almost unfathomable for us to imagine that for lack of $700 she has suffered like this.

God save our world.....or more appropriately, may God use us to save our world.

On October 6, Mme. Georges had her tumor removal operation. Later that day we received this news:

> *April:*
> *Thanks for sending her to us. She has been a   delight. We removed all gross tumors....She could not live the way she was though. She is recovering slowly. She is eating now and up and about. She will need another fairly big operation to close the big hole in the neck. We are waiting for the wound to heal a bit before doing that.*
> *Dick*

What a time of celebration. We had finally seen all of the efforts we had put in to trying to help this woman finally pay off. On October 17, Mme. Georges had her wound closed and a pectoralis myocutaneous (the area on the upper chest) flap skin graft skin was placed over the open wound area where the tumor had been removed. She remained at HAS for an additional 2 weeks recovering until she was able to return home on October 31. She returned a few weeks later for a follow up and Dick felt she was doing just fine with good healing and no signs of infection.

On November 14, just before Thanksgiving that year, I received this email from Dick:

> *April:*
> *She came to clinic today. She went first over to the surgery ward to show off to everyone how good she looks. I took out her sutures today. She is granulating a   few of the corners of the reconstruction but functionally is normal except for a bit of a hoarse voice. She doesn't have to hide anymore and she is really grateful for you providing her this opportunity.*
> *Dick*

What could we say? Except... "Praise to the Lord the Almighty the King of Creation. Oh, my soul praise Him for He is our help and salvation" (Joachim Neander, 1863).

The strength the Lord gave us to persevere had literally changed a life. Someone was made whole because of the love and care of the team of medical workers who went to help in Haiti that summer. The team and some from our church picked up the cost of the surgery and hospital expenses. All in all it was less than $2000. Just $2000 to change this woman's life- small change to most of us-but life changing for her.

That was the second story in the nomination for the MLK Community Caregiver Award.

Before surgery   **After surgery**

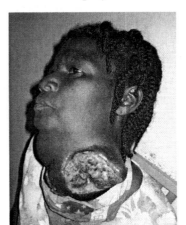
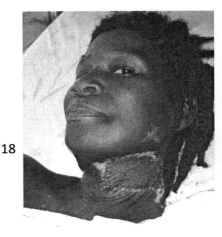

18

Time went by and the date that the award was to be announced was set-January 12, 2010. I had been selected as one of the eight finalists for the award. Prior to the ceremony, the committee wanted to make short videos of each nominee to be shown at the awards ceremony. I went at my appointed time. They had provided us with the questions that would be asked so we could be prepared with our answers for the taping. They asked me to describe the situation of us sending Romel to medical school in my own words and also asked me to tell the story of Mme Georges. During the final version of the video, they would show pictures of me and others working in Haiti.

I read the nomination summaries of the other nominees at the video session. As I did, I thought about what stiff competition I was up against, one woman had facilitated teaching workshop for those supporting family members who were mentally ill for 25 years; another who had worked on numerous Habitat projects. And yet another who had done community health work with the disadvantaged and underserved populations in the local community.

As the day for the award approached, I really didn't give it a lot of thought. I was provided several invitations and asked my parents and a few close friends to attend.

At noon on January 12, 2010, we all gathered in a lovely convention hall at Duke Hospital for the awards ceremony. The organizers had sent out an email to all of the nominees explaining what the program would entail and how things would be done. They explained that they would name each nominee, show their video and then present them with a plaque commemorating their nomination. After that was completed they would announce the winner from all of the nominees. They specifically indicated that the nominees would not be announced in any particular order.

As the nominees were each announced, their videos played and they received their plaques, I was relishing in the accomplishments of each one. There were only two left. When the other person's name was announced, I remember thinking, why did they put me last. I wish I had been earlier.

However, after that person received her plaque, Dr. Fulkerson, the chief operating officer of Duke Hospital, said: "And now we will see the video of the winner of the 2010 Martin Luther King Community Caregiver Award".

The next thing I saw on the screen was "April Perry-Luke's Mission". I then heard my own words as I saw myself on the screen:

"I really believe that we are called to help the poor and the needy so I went on a mission trip to Haiti. I thought it might be a place where I could help people in need. And as I have worked there I do believe it has been something that has helped transform them and has transformed me....

We work with translators in our clinic and my translator's was someone who lived in the slum that we were working in. It was clear to me that he had great potential he had a dream of trying to do something in health care but just didn't have the resources to do that. We have been able to put him through medical school over the last seven years and on Monday I am leaving to go to Haiti to attend his graduation.

So this is a young man who would really had no future, no life and now actually has the potential to serve his community and support his family and his country through providing health care to them...

Last year when we went on a mission trip we had came across a woman who had a very, very large tumor about the size of a soccer ball on her neck. She had had it for at least eight years. We didn't feel like it was cancer but it was clearly going to kill her if it kept on growing. Besides that, it was very infected very obnoxious and she was quite stigmatized by the community because of this.

We found out that Dick McCann, a Duke surgeon, was doing a sabbatical in Haiti. We were able to get the woman down to him to get her evaluated and he was able to get the tumor off and performed a couple of skin grafts and now she is living very well without any recurrences of the tumor. It has just been a life changing thing for her. She is now living a normal life. People treat her normally...

I would encourage everybody just to open your eyes and look around you for the needs around you. I will say first off you don't have to travel to a foreign country to do this. There are needs in your community, in your neighborhood; there are needs in your church. There are many, many needs here in Durham, NC...

I think my life has been completely transformed and will continue to be transformed as I continue to follow the calling of the Lord in my life through serving people..."

It was clear to me then that I had won. I was in shock. As I watched my own video play, I realized I had better think of something to say and quickly.

I took out a pen and jotted two things down-
1. If everybody helped a few people—and
2. $5K will go far in Haiti.

"April Perry, the 2010 Martin Luther King Community Caregiver Award Winner.' Dr. Fulkerson said.

As the video finished and I was announced as the winner, I was asked to come up to the stage to receive award and the check.

Of course, the obligatory photos were taken of me with the COO of the hospital and the check. He then asked me if I wanted to say a few words.

As best I can remember it, this is what I said:

"I am truly honored to be recognized among these other nominees each of whom has done amazing things in the community for those in need. I don't really consider myself extraordinary. What I have done is to try to help a few people within my own world. Now if everyone in this room and everyone in this hospital and health system started to help a few people within their own world—something extraordinary would begin to happen and we could all be a part of that.

I am so grateful that the administration has chosen to honor us with this substantial gift. It shows not only that they honor our work but are willing to invest in it to move it forward. In a country where most attempt to survive on $1 per day, $5000 will go a very long way.

Thanks again to the administration, to Carol Ann Mullis who nominated me and to the other nominees for their wonderful work with those less fortunate than ourselves. I am privileges that the Lord has called me to work in Haiti and I want to continue to be faithful to that calling. Thank you. "

To say I was elated would be an understatement. While getting the recognition was nice, all I could think about was what $5,000 could do for our ministry. We hadn't even considered that I might win. It was just a nice thing to be recognized at some level and allow the story of the Haitian people to be told yet again to more people who might not have heard. When I was that big check for $5,000, all I could think of was that $5,000 was a fortune in Haiti.

I spent the rest of the hour celebrating and taking even more pictures with my family and friends, collecting the flowers and other memorabilia that were a part of that day. And about 1:45 PM we all left to return to our places of work.

As I returned to my office, it was shortly after 2 PM. The word had already made it back and people were waiting at the front door congratulating me, and wishing me well. There were already several emails and voice mails of congratulations. News like this travels fast. It was a really joyous time. But that was the last joy I was to feel for my work in Haiti for quite some time to come.

About 4:10 PM, I got a pop up news alert notification on my computer monitor from my online news service that there had been a severe earthquake in Haiti.

All of our lives were about to change forever.

Chapter 2
His Crushing Mercy

The early pictures coming in from Port au Prince looked really bad. Even though I didn't expect to see the kind of buildings one would see here, and I knew that this was a third world country, the pictures told the story that this was an enormous disaster.

We watched the morning news shows and saw the Montana Hotel, a hotel I had been to on a couple of occasions and knew well, laying literally in ruins. This hotel is where anyone who is of any importance usually stays while they are in Port au Prince. There are only a couple of hotels in Port au Prince that would be what most Americans think of when we say the word "hotel". Most mission teams stay in guest houses. These are simple facilities that usually have dorm style rooms, a dining room where meals are served and shared bathrooms. The ones we have stayed in have been clean and comfortable, but not fancy.

However, the Hotel Montana would be comparable in Haiti to the Ritz Carlton in New York City. It is a lovely hotel even by third world standards. The lobby and restaurant are all open air, something very common in tropical countries. It overlooked the city so dining there in the evening, which I had done one time, was a pleasant experience. The rooms were comparable to a four star hotel here in the states and had most of the amenities that one would expect, including air conditioning, a rare luxury in Haiti.

The United Methodist Church had a personal interest in the collapse of the Hotel Montana. The director of foreign missions for the entire UMC denomination was in Haiti at the time of the earthquake with several colleagues from the denomination as well. His name was Sam Dixon. I had read on our church website that he was listed as missing and there was deep concern for his safety. They were actively working to rescue people from the Montana. I had seen that on the cable news. I prayed he might be one of the ones that they found alive and could rescue.

Additionally, a friend had told me of a colleague's father who was in Haiti then leading a mission team of college students from Dunn College. They were staying at the Montana as well. No one had heard from them either.

As I watched the news footage that day, I saw more and more areas that I recognized from having been in Port au Prince so many times. Each time I saw a place or an area that I knew personally, and the destruction associated with it, the enormity and impact of the situation began to sink deeper within my psyche.

I sensed myself slowly building a soft shell of denial, or at least protective emotional cushioning, thinking that somehow, by some miracle, the people we knew wouldn't be affected by this crisis. I needed to gather the information about this. It was clear at that time that this would affect our ministry-how I wasn't really sure yet-but we needed to have information in order to make decisions about the impact of this on our work.

I sent emails again to all of those in Haiti affiliated with our ministry. I asked them to please contact us just as soon as they could just let us know they were alive. As predictions of the death toll started out at 20,000 and progressed upwards to possibly over 100,000 in the first 24 hours, I became aware, in some emotionally distant way, that it was highly likely that people we knew had lost their lives. But I was still hopeful.

Having been through a crisis like this with the people of Haiti in 2004 when the rebels were taking over the country and threatening the capital city, I had already experienced then the sense of helplessness that was, now yet again, forming in my inner soul. Watching people I had come to know and love dearly experience a life threatening crisis from afar and feeling like I couldn't do anything about it but just watch the situation unfold is a terrible feeling. Twenty four/seven access to news and world events directly on the ground has provided us with wonderful opportunities to know things in real time. However, in this kind of situation that one thing we could do was pray.

As Christians we often think of prayer as a last resort when really it should be our first response to any situation. Praying as a last resort is so contrary to the teaching of Jesus and the apostle Paul and others in the New Testament. Hebrews 4:14-16 tells us we can pray boldly -- "That is why we have a great High Priest who has gone to heaven, Jesus the Son of God. Let us cling to him and never stop trusting him. This High Priest of ours understands our weaknesses, for he faced all of the same temptations we do, yet he did not sin. So let us come boldly to the throne of our gracious God. There we will receive his mercy, and we will find grace to help us when we need it."

James reminds us to pray with sincerity, honor, and humbleness before the Almighty God. "The earnest prayer of a righteous person has great power and wonderful results" (James 5:16). Finally in the Old Testament, the writer of Daniel in Chapter 9 verse 18 tells us: "We do not ask because we deserve help, but because you are so merciful." In this verse, Mercy means showing favor, compassion, and kindness. We can count on God to show compassion and mercy on us when we come before Him in prayer.

My own thoughts on prayer are that I don't really understand it completely. I have studied it some throughout my Christian journey. I do realize that it is a tremendous gift. However, not understanding it, I do it because we are instructed by Jesus to pray. I believe that the Holy Spirit who is our intercessor, will take our prayers, no matter how eloquent, simple or confusing, and bring them to the Father in a way that allows Him to respond to the cries of our heart-whether that we cries of praise, thanksgiving, mourning, questioning or requests for help of some kind we can't readily define.

So, on that Wednesday morning, less than 18 hours after the earthquake, I found myself emailing my pastor and asking if we could lead a prayer vigil the next evening for the people affected by the earthquake in Haiti. Shelia and I had done this in the past during the 2004 rebellion and coup in Haiti so we had a format in mind. It would take very little to put it together. But we wanted people to know about it so they could come. We needed to decide early in the day if it were to happen the next evening.

By 9 AM I had received an email response that he thought this was a great idea and for us to move forward with it. I agreed to do the draft of the program and send it to him later that day to look at.

In our previous prayer vigil, we had wanted to help people pray in a way that was meaningful to them. Although we know the Lord hears our prayers, no matter how confusing they may seem to us, we have found that personalizing these situations helps to bring it closer to people.

I pulled out the format from the previous one. My heart was actually saddened as it brought back reminders to me of that very dark time in our work in Haiti and the terror that my friends there experienced over those months. I also thought of the people we knew who lost their lives to the violence which followed Aristide's exit from the country and the resulting years of instability.

Most of it we would use again. The format was designed to give participants a scripture to meditate upon, and then allow time for silent prayers or prayers out loud based upon the theme of that scripture. These are called Bidding prayers. I like this format

27

and it has worked effectively for me other times when I have used it.

As Wednesday passed, I received calls from several reporters who somehow knew of our ministry in Haiti and wanted to get a local perspective on the situation. I mentioned the prayer vigil to all of them and asked them to please announce it in their own form of media.

I updated our website to allow people who were interested specifically in our ministry to see how those affiliated with our ministry had fared. Even as I listed the names of the people we were especially concerned with, I remembered those that I didn't know who had lost their lives.

The images of the Hotel Montana wouldn't leave my mind. I knew that there had to have been a lot of people in that hotel at four in the afternoon. When I saw the pile of rubble that used to be the hotel, it was hard for me to imagine that anyone would be able to survive that. I have seen extraordinary rescues from other building collapses. My mind's eye was hoping for that, but it was clear to me that the collapse of the hotel Montana and the resulting loss of life, was representative of what this disaster would mean to the country of Haiti.

As I tried to think about how the country of Haiti would respond to this on every level-disaster preparedness, nonexistent in Haiti since the country is in a constant state of low level disaster, dealing with the injured and dead with an extremely poor baseline health care system, rebuilding a non functional government pre-earthquake. It was really hard for me to even grasp how that would work in this country where on a good day I would describe the government and governmental agencies as extremely dysfunctional.

When asked by a colleague early on Wednesday morning what did I think about this, all I could respond was "I just don't know how this is going to play itself out".

Wednesday was a day of considerably anxiety. We couldn't reach anyone in Haiti and neither could anyone else. The cable and network news indicated that all cell phone service, the main stay of telephone service in Haiti, was non functional due to damage to the cell towers.

At the same time, I was getting emails of congratulations from many people on winning the award. Everywhere I turned at work, someone was hugging me and congratulating me on winning the award. On Wednesday morning I got two very poignant emails from two dear former colleagues who I had worked closely with in Pediatric Cardiology. Their words were a balm to me.

> *Dear April*
> *I was planning on writing you today to congratulate you on winning the MLK award, but after news events regarding Haiti have appeared, I am certain your thoughts are only on your friends who are suffering there. I am so sorry to hear of this news and cannot imagine the devastation that has taken   place. I feel certain you will soon be on your way soon if at all possible to lend a hand. Please be safe   and take care.*
> *Carol*
> ~~~~~
>
> *April -*
> *I initially started out writing this email to congratulate you on the MLK community caregiver award (kudos to you!). However, I just read on the net about the devastation in Haiti from the earthquake. I am sure our thoughts and prayers are with your friends and colleagues there. Know I am thinking about you - please let me know if I can do anything.*
>
> *Take care – B*

I was grateful that someone had acknowledged or at least recognized the conflict that was being generated within me. On the one hand, I was so thrilled at receiving this great gift for our work in Haiti, only to find out that within two hours, terrible devastation had hit those same people for which we were rejoicing. Of course, I was terribly worried about all of the people in Haiti, especially those that I knew. I was also concerned deeply about the future. Just how would they ever rebuild? Where would the help come from? Would anybody even care? And then, having to deal with the difficulty of the emotional roller coaster that I was on - going from elation at one minute to deep sorrow in the next.

I tried to work but my mind was elsewhere. The responses from people ranged from "Oh I just can't imagine how terrible this might make you feel" to the opposite end of the spectrum "Wasn't there an earthquake or something in Haiti recently?' Yeah—*or something.*

By day's end, we had the prayer vigil nearly all planned in order to give to the church secretary that evening to make the programs up for the following evening. We have a Wednesday night supper followed by a prayer meeting. This is my favorite service of the week. As I entered the fellowship hall to eat, many people came up to me and acknowledged how terrible the earthquake was and offered their prayers and support for the Haitians and us. At the table where we paid was a bright neon green paper which listed ways that this body of Christ could help the earthquake victims of Haiti. It gave specific contribution information for large reputable aid agencies like the Red Cross, the United Methodist Relief Organization and Samaritans Purse. It also listed the ingredients for hygiene packets that the United Methodist Relief Organization was asking for and how to assemble them. Directions were given on where to drop them at the church for pick up each week by the relief group.

30

In our prayer meeting we had a specific time of prayer for the earthquake victims and those of us who worked in Haiti. It was a moving time. Additionally, the prayer vigil was announced and all were invited and instructed to invite anyone who was interested.

My heart was very heavy as I went to bed that night. I had checked my email so many times that day with no word from anyone. I didn't really expect that email would be a priority in a catastrophe like this, but I had hoped to hear something from someone, we wanted someone to tell us more about what was happening on the ground there than we could see from what the news was showing.

Thursday morning brought more images that were hard to stomach. Many of the scenes were so familiar to me. I recognized specific streets, the presidential palace, the market area which now looked more like a war zone or a bombed out ghetto. I saw entire blocks where many merchants and commerce centered itself, now nearly completely leveled.

It was hard to imagine areas of the city that weren't impacted from what we were seeing on the screen. The earthquake was the all-consuming story on all of the cable shows and pretty much dominated all of the local networks as well. Many of the local stations were trying to find local angles to the Haiti story.

There are a lot of people in this local area who do mission work in Haiti. Many are affiliated with Duke Medical Center. That morning I received calls from two reporters asking if they could come to the prayer vigil and report it on the TV and in the newspaper. They also wanted to talk to me. I cleared this with our pastor and thought it might be something that would promote the cause of Christ. I spoke clearly to the reporters that we would allow them to come but they could not interrupt us or the people there as it was first and foremost a worship service.

I continued to update our website, letting people know that we had heard virtually nothing from anyone in Haiti. We were concerned about the medical student we sponsored, Edmund Franz, the doctor we supported who was finishing up his residency and his family who lived right in Port au Prince, a number of translators and friends, Eddy, Jules, Emmanuel, Sonel and our ministry partner Pastor Jean Revil. In addition we were deeply concerned about the two nuns who were close friends to us who lived about 30 miles from Port au Prince, Sister Carmelle and Sister Simone. They ran an orphanage with 52 children.

It was really hard to tell from the news reports how, if at all, areas outside of the direct city were affected. I guess my hope was that the farther away they were from the epicenter, the better off they might be. Additionally, we also knew that there was a mission team in Fondwa where our dear sister friends lived, and were concerned about them. Given that it was a very mountainous area, I was deeply concerned about their welfare and the welfare of the 52 orphaned children.

I was trying to work at my desk, when a nurse colleague named Karen came into my office. I was on the phone when she came in and when I got off, I saw her writing a note. She said that she was just going to leave me a note but she wanted to touch base with me this very difficult morning.

Karen has been a missionary for a number of years and was now working stateside for a few years. She worked with some very good friends of mine, also missionaries, in an eastern European country doing public health, water and hygiene projects. She knows poverty of this nature and the kinds of difficulties that the Haitian people face on a daily basis. She also knows what it is like to love people like this in the same way I did.

She started "I just wanted to see you this morning. I can't imagine what you are going through. I just wanted you to know that I think it must so hard to realize how wonderful it was to win that award on Tuesday only to be devastated within hours about this terrible tragedy."

She continued. "It is such a paradox. The Lord has granted you such a wonderful joy and followed it immediately with such a terrible sorrow. It must be like experiencing 'severe grace' or 'crushing mercy'. That is the only way I can imagine what you must be feeling right now".

Karen has such command of words. She often amazes me with the eloquence that she uses to express herself. This isn't the last you will hear of her in this book. I thanked her for being so perceptive and having such insight. Yes, that was really what I was feeling-severe grace; crushing mercy. I wouldn't forget that.

We hugged, she had to hurry off but I knew I had felt a kindred spirit in her.

I tried to continue to work when at 9:45 AM an email came in that a friend had forwarded to me from the head of a ministry that we had worked with in the past. I was so happy to hear something so I opened up the email and began to read.

He described the situation as "critical". He said that he and his wife were unharmed and their house standing and mostly undamaged. They lived right in the middle of Port au Prince.

Most people were living with

> *"lots of fear thinking that the last days are here. Some people heard on the news that this ordeal (assuming he meant further aftershocks) would last 'until Friday... No one wants to get close to their homes for fear of death...thinking that their house would fall on them. We have over three million people living in Port-au-Prince most of them have been sleeping on the streets since the*

warning. I'm sure some of them would continue to do that even beyond Friday, the supposed last day of the quake, for fear of death."

At least they were safe. They lived right in the middle of the city so I continued to have hope that many people we knew were still safe.
His email went on:

"Cells phone are practically dead except for one c company (Haitel)[few people used that service]... Gas is very scarce and very expensive. One gallon of gas cost as much as $12.50 (U.S. dollars) in some places yesterday. Some people are taking advantage of the situation to practice black market. Markets aren't open; food is scarce, expensive and rare, gas stations aren't open either. Water trucks are not delivering water. Schools and businesses are closed. It was a very unusual day in Haiti yesterday. It sounds like what John talked about in Revelation is begging to be a reality at least for a short time in Haiti."

The reality began to hit me that this was clearly as bad as what I might have thought from the beginning but was hoping it wouldn't be.

He continued:

"Yesterday, I was able to visit several families in their homes. Their situation demands much attention. Many houses are destroyed; some need major repairs, lots of them need to be totally rebuilt. So far we've registered five deaths in the three churches that I visited and many injured people. In the case of the Repatriate church, the quake started while there were having 278 people showed up for Bible study and prayer. Many people were injured while trying to run to save their lives. It

34

was a sad thing to see. One young boy, about 8 years old, died from a fallen wall while getting ready to go to church. Several got injured. Our church compounds are being used as places of refuge, away from the danger of any houses and trees that could fall on the people. Thank God for the soccer field in [the church compounds].... Both are being used as camping grounds for the people in the community."

Again, I felt extreme sadness but also hope seeing that churches and community areas were being used for places of gathering. Finally, he said:

"Some of you might remember Boselor, known to some of you as Bosie, he was found died [dead] *yesterday inside a class room with several other students where he used to go to school."*

These were the words that I had braced myself from having to hear.

Bosie was dead.

Boselor, or Bosie as he was known to us, was an accomplished translator. He lived in Cite Soleil, the slum where we worked and provided medical care with our medical teams in our early work in Haiti. As time went along we became good friends. Shelia had Bosie as her translator for the last two trips that we made to Haiti. Bosie had worked for us for about eight years. He was one of the regular groups of translators that we had when I took teams to Haiti. Each time I came to Haiti I always tried to see him at church or another place.

He was studying to become an accountant. He wanted so much to be able to support himself and his family and was working diligently to try to do that. And now, Bosie was dead.

My heart was broken. The situation I had hoped so much that wouldn't occur but knew somewhere deep down that it would have occurred.

Bosie was dead. And there would likely be more.

Given that they were predicting that 100,000 people had died, it was hard to imagine that those we knew and loved would not be touched.

Now I was really scared.

Was Sister Carmelle dead, too? What about Romel, our newly graduated physician? Was his wife Fregga, who lived in the city dead? His family? Other translators, Eddy, Jules, Dennis, Edmund our other student and other friends? Were they dead too? The children at the orphanage? The mission team? Pastor Jean Revil-our ministry partner. The thoughts were too much to bear.

I am not sure exactly what happened during the next few minutes. I know I stopped reading the email there. I wept uncontrollably with my head in my hands. A colleague in an adjacent office must have heard me and came in to see what was happened. She then went to get a couple of other colleagues of mine who came in to see what was wrong.

I called Shelia immediately at work. I asked her if she had someone with her because I had bad news from Haiti. She said her officemate was there. What was it? I read her the email.
She was clearly upset and tearful immediately. She asked me if the email had mentioned anyone else. I really didn't know because I stopped reading there. She asked me to send it to her and said she would call me back.

My friends gathered about me as I wept with tears of shear grief. How much more could these people be expected to take? Why did they have to suffer so, so, so much? Would it ever end for the poor people of Haiti?

My friend Carol Ann, the one who had spearheaded the nomination process for the award, suggested that I just go home. It was pointless to try to work. She even offered to drive me. But I assured her I could drive but didn't want to go home to an empty house.

I called my Mom, who lives in the same city about 5 minutes from my work. I told her, crying as I said it, that I had bad news from Haiti and I was coming over to their house.

Her response stunned me "Come on over. I have been expecting this."

She had expected to hear news like this. She had prepared herself for this kind of thing.

I spent the first part of the afternoon with her and my Dad trying to believe what my eyes had read and trying to hang on to the smallest amount of hope that others didn't succumb to the same fate. The rest of the afternoon I sat at home partially numb and trying to get ready for the prayer vigil, while mourning and sporadically weeping over Bosie's death, worried over who else might have died or been seriously injured. Things were hitting home now.

Earlier that morning, I had made arrangements to meet with a TV reporter at the church prior to the prayer vigil. I explained to him and the cameraman again that we didn't want them pointing the camera in people faces while they were worshipping or distracting from the service. The camera man said he understood but in order for people to really see what we were doing and to bring attention to this event, it would be important for him to get some other shots. My skepticism with media is strong but I had to trust that he would honor our wishes. When he interviewed

37

me, he asked if I knew anyone who had been seriously injured or had died as a result of the earthquake. It was the first time I told someone else about Bosie. Yes, this terrible thing had happened to individual people not just to a "country".

After the interview, Shelia and I had made up slips of paper with individual people's names on them that we knew from Haiti who might be affected. Our intention was to have people take one or two prior to the service. At the time that we appointed, they would have the opportunity to pray aloud for the person/people on the papers. It would give them a specific name of someone on the ground in Haiti right now that needed their prayers. We named all of our friends and ministry partners there as well as the UN peace keeping force, the aid workers and the Haitian government.

As we were preparing for the prayer vigil in one of the rooms of the church, our pastor brought in an email he had just gotten from the husband of the team leader in Fondwa. He knew them both from Divinity school. The team leader's husband's name was David. In the email he said he had not heard from his wife Jamlyn, the team leader, but that he considered that something to be cautiously optimistic about at this time. His thinking was that as an American with a group of Americans in Haiti right now, Jamlyn would have the perspective that we were having. She knew how concerned everyone her in the US would be and if there were problems, he felt she would move heaven and earth to notify us. Because of her responsibility for the team, he had to believe that she was looking after their needs first even if it gave us a level of increased anxiety.

I understood his thinking. I just didn't happen to completely agree with it. That is the kind of thinking I would have if I was a team leader in a situation like this. I would want to use every resource to let people know we were safe and then just wait until we could get out. However, given the events earlier in the day and the stark reality I had been faced with, that people we did know were now dead as Shelia had predicted less than 24 hours earlier, I hesitated to be as optimistic.

The appointed time came for the prayer vigil. There were actually two news crews and three newspaper reporters there. To think that prayer would get so much press was amazing. The film and camera crews were sensitive to the situation. The sanctuary was nearly filled. There were people from the community as well as people from our local church.

We began with a reading of Isaiah 58, a place to set the tone. God is pointing out to Israel and us what He really wants to see in our "fasting" or service to and worship to Him, that taking care of the poor, hungry, the naked and those who are oppressed. I led this section. I challenged myself and others there to think about how we had treated those in need and how we had perhaps not met the expectation of God with regard to our concerns for other.

Shelia read passages from Psalm 46. Our pastors both participated with scripture passages on confession of our own sins of neglect of the poor and assurances of forgiveness. Then we offered people a time to pray for those in Haiti that they had picked from the basket. Through tear filled eyes, I announced that we had just heard today of the death of one of our beloved friends Bosie Souffrant. We knew someone had his name so we asked whoever had Bosie's name to please thank God for his life and instead pray for his family.

As they called out their names and prayed for them out loud, the tears flowed from both Shelia and me. It was, as many times has been described in the Old Testament, a crying out to the Lord. Please, please, God have mercy on your faithful children in Haiti. Their faith is so strong. Their love for you has taught me so much about you. Please, we cried out, have mercy on them. Give them strength and courage to endure this terrible time.

When the vigil was finished, we departed separately in an atmosphere of grief and solitude. I was gathering some things up at the front of the church, when a young man who I didn't recognize came up to me. He introduced himself as John McCann from the Durham Herald Sun, our local newspaper. He wondered if I had a few minutes I could talk to him.

He apologized for feeling intrusive at an emotional time like this but he really wanted to talk more about the vigil. He asked for the specific scripture references that we used and why we picked them. He asked what the impact of hearing about Bosie's death had had on me this particular day.

After a few more questions, he looked at me and said, "The spirit at Aldersgate Methodist Church tonight was so special. Is it always like this here?"

I said, "Yes, this is common in this particular body of Christ."

He got my contact information and asked if he could call me later and then left. Later I was to find out that John McCann is a well known regular columnist at the paper. Since I don't read the paper, I didn't know him. But all of my friends who read the paper regularly are very familiar with him. He is a conservative Christian and often presents that point of view in his columns. He is well respected and is allowed the freedom to write his thoughts because of the solid reputation he has built.

Let me interject here, I wasn't thrilled with this personal attention from the media. I have had dealings with the media before. Several times in my life I have found myself being interview by local press because of my involvement in high profile events both in my personal and professional life. I have a healthy skepticism about the media. But I also realized that a situation like this would provide an opportunity for me to tell a very wide audience the story of the people of Haiti and make them aware of the personal nature of this devastation on individual people and our work there.

When these opportunities arose, I decided to ask the Lord to try to help what I say raise awareness of the great needs that exist in Haiti on a good day and to try to let people understand how desperate the situation is now. I really had a heartfelt desire to help people come to know the Haitians as I had, to let them see these people that they view on a story on CNN or through a slide show on Yahoo as real people, individuals that I know personally and have come to love. I wanted them to know that I knew people who had died there and others I loved whose status I didn't know yet.

Each evening I would update our website with any news I had on any of our friends or ministry partners. We kept up with other website from ministries that we knew of and how things were faring with their particular work there, as well as to get any information we could. I was also careful not to post anything that I had not been able to confirm. So many rumors or partial information was being distributed. It was important not to propagate more anxiety in this already anxiety ridden situation.

My heart was heavy that evening as I updated the website. I found a picture of Bosie and Shelia on our last trip where he served as her translator. It brought back so many wonderful memories of him, but also intense grief knowing that he was now in eternity with his Maker. I decided to put a memorial on the home page of the website so that anyone visiting our site would first see him and know of our love for him, gratitude for his work with us, and deep sorrow at his untimely death. We hadn't heard any other information that day and prayed tomorrow would bring some better news from those we loved in Haiti.

I began a blog on a new page entitled Earthquake Updates. I would list the people that we knew and update their status as we found information out.

As I closed my blog that night, I found myself remembering the conversation with Karen earlier in the day. It seemed like ages ago as I sat there in the midst of the late evening. Had it only been eight hours earlier she said to me "It must feel like severe grace or crushing mercy". So much had happened since then.

Before I realized it, unconsciously, I found myself closing my blog entry with the phrase "Under His crushing mercy, April".

Yes, it felt like crushing mercy. I stopped right then and prayed for crushing mercy for my beloved Haitian people as well.

It had been a long and draining day for me. Before going to bed I decided to check my email one final time to see if there was any news from our friends in Haiti about their status.

The Lord was so gracious. He provided me comfort in the love and support of people here for our situation.

The first one was from a friend at church who was scheduled to go to Jamaica in three weeks on a mission team from our church. He referenced the people in the prayer card he received during the prayer vigil.

> *"April:*
> *Please let me tell you how saddened Mary, my disciple class, the Jamaica Mission Team, and I are about the disasters in Haiti! I will continue to pray for the safety and health of Sister Carmelle, the Fondwa orphanage, school administrators and all the children. Please let me know when you hear of their whereabouts! If we can come up with some money for relief, can you help with the dispersal so that the people that need it receive it?*
> *Steve"*

One of my friends on the Jamaica Mission Team told me they

were meeting that evening but had moved their meeting and their Bible study so that they could all attend the prayer vigil. Steve was one of those people.

Another came from my dear friends in California. Alex and Debbie had traveled to Haiti with us two times. Their hearts were with the people of Haiti. They have such servant's hearts and had been a source of strength and encouragement for me for years as we worked in Haiti. They had kept up with our work even after moving to Los Angeles. The day they moved was a very sad day in my life.

> *"April*
> *I don't know what to write. We were in tears when we heard   of Bosie's death. Hard though it is to hear news, thank you for sending it. We are praying for you. I feel helpless.*
> *Love*
> *Debbie and Alex "*

I was so grateful for the love and support emails like this provided. I was to find out that the love and support they provided through the ministry of the Holy Spirit would sustain me through even more difficult times that lay ahead.

Boselor Souffrant
1982-2010

43

Chapter 3
A Report from Fondwa

Each day since Tuesday evening, the day the earthquake happened, I had found that dawn would bring with it many new and difficult challenges and an occasional joy. This day was to be no exception.

A number of years ago, during the aftermath of Hurricane Katrina, I registered with two disaster relief organizations to be placed on their list of available medical staff in the event they needed people--NC Baptist Men and Samaritan's Purse. Both are top notch relief organizations. I had received a number of requests from NC Baptist Men over the past few years but none of them ever panned out.

Late on Thursday evening, I emailed the director of the volunteers to just let him know that I was still available if they were going to send a team to Haiti. I also made contact with my friend at Samaritan's Purse and told her the same thing. She wrote back that they would definitely be sending a team and thought with my experience in Haiti I would be an asset to a team they would send. She told me if I didn't hear from them by week's end to contact her again.

I woke up early, (I hadn't been able to sleep well), and decided to just get up. I watched the report the TV stations did on the prayer vigil and was deeply moved at how sensitively they covered it. The pictures were very poignant--people around the altar praying and a video of hands reaching into a basket to choose names of people in Haiti to pray for.

Additionally, the local newspaper ran two stories on it. Both were very good and the copies presented the deep concern of all that were there.

As I opened my email that morning, there was one that immediately caught my attention. It was from Romel. Oh, how happy I was just to see his name on the "from" column. I knew he had to be at least alive if there was an email from him.
It read;

> *April,*
> *I am alive but cannot find my parents or Fregga. Please pray for us.*
> *Romel, MD.*

That was all it said but for now, it was enough. I ran upstairs where Shelia was showering and told her that we had heard from Romel and what he said. I will admit to a bit of frustration at him not saying more, but I had the most important information I needed--that he was alive.

However, once I realized exactly what the email said, I became very worried again. This was an emotional roller coaster; feelings of profound gratitude and elation at even the smallest amount of good news only to realize within seconds that there was no news of others, causing even more anxiety and concern.
Romel couldn't locate his parents or wife. He was doing his residency in Les Cayes, which is about 30 miles from Port au Prince. From what we could discern on the maps, it seemed to be an area which, if affected at all, was only mildly affected. We had hoped he was there but didn't know for sure. His family and wife, on the other hand, were living right in the middle of Port au Prince in the areas that were at the epicenter. We had been so worried about them and now had even more reason to worry. Romel himself couldn't find them.

I immediately sent out an email to those close to our ministry letting them know that Romel was alive and that we had heard from them. I asked them to pray for his family and wife, Fregga that they would be found alive.

Just then the phone rang. It was about 10:00 AM. I was working from home and wondered who might be calling me at this time. While I often screen my calls when I am preoccupied, I decided to answer this one, thinking perhaps it was someone from Haiti trying to reach me.

The caller identified herself as Lisa Clarke, the Missions Committee Chairman for my local Church, Aldersgate United Methodist Church. Lisa was also the team leader for one of our upcoming Jamaica Mission team. We were sending two teams this year and hers was scheduled to leave in a month or so.

She asked me if I had a minute to talk and I said of course. She went on to tell me how moved she and others had been at the prayer vigil the night before. She indicated that having specific people to pray for was a very meaningful experience for her.

The Jamaica Mission team had met following the service for their regular meeting. I remembered her telling me that they had delayed the start of their meeting so they could participate in the prayer vigil. She then went on to tell me that the entire team had discussed this situation at the meeting and they had unanimously decided they were going to delay their upcoming mission trip to Jamaica and instead donate all the funds they had raised for that trip to Luke's Mission to be used for earthquake relief. She also told me that all of the proceeds for their upcoming silent auction- normally a very large fund raising event for the Jamaica mission team, would all be going to Luke's Mission for Haiti relief.

Of course I was astonished at this response. But I wanted to talk with her more before this went any further. I knew that people felt terrible for the people affected in Haiti but Jamaica had needs as well and I wasn't confident that taking money from one group of poor people to give to another was the right thing to do. I expressed my concern about this and asked her to please think

46

about this some more and we could pray about it together before they made a final decision.

She said the decision was final. They had talked about this and would be "delaying" their trip. They would continue on with their proposed mission trip but later in the year. The team had discussed this and felt that the people they worked with in Jamaica would support this decision. They would still send the second team but this larger team would be using their resources to help the people of Haiti. They felt like the people of Haiti needed this now. And their work with Jamaica would continue-- just be delayed. No one felt there was a sense of urgency about the Jamaican work like there was with the situation in Haiti.

Of course I was overwhelmed at the sacrifice that this group of people was making. One of them had sent me the email the evening before which touched my heart deeply. To think that they would delay the trip that they had planned for nearly a year was overwhelming to me. The desire to help so much that they would give all of the money from their upcoming fund raiser to the cause of the earthquake showed a love and a level of concern that I wasn't really accustomed to.

I expressed my thanks as well as I could and was happy inside for the good news. I really didn't know how to respond and it wouldn't be until much later that the real impact of this tremendous gift would be clear to all of us.

When I hung up the phone, I went back to my computer. I noticed also, in my email inbox an email with the subject message-*News from Fondwa*. I clicked on that to see what news might have occurred overnight. A mutual friend had received the following text message from Jamelyn Williams, the mission team leader who was in Fondwa at the time of the earthquake.

> *Hello Friends and Family--*
> *Our team is in Leogane, Haiti. We arrived today after*
> *taking motorcycles down the mountain from Fondwa.*

*The road is completely covered in dirt. Everyone is safe
and healthy...*
*Sadly, Fondwa has been hit hard. The guesthouse is in
ruins   and so is the school. Jesula's house is gone too.
The Sisters lost one of their own in the community--
Sister Oudel. We also lost Jude--he was the young baby
and he was with Sister Oudel.*
*Dr. Delson lost the second story of his house. We are
staying at Hospital St.Croix [in Leogane] tonight. The
guesthouse is gone but we will sleep with John and
Susie Parker [caretakers of the Hopital St. Croix guest
houser. Tomorrow morning we will go to the
Embassy and wait for US Aid plane to help bring us
home.*
*Please continue to pray for us. I am so sorry this has
been   so difficult on all of you. We have been praying
that God's grace will cover you and offer you peace.
Lot of love,
Jamelyn and the team*

Again, that emotional roller coaster. The mission team was OK
but Baby Jude was dead as was Sister Oudel. Oh how my heart
ached and yet I was joyful at the same time.

I was reminded of the scripture text in Ezra 3.

*"And all the people gave a great shout of praise to the LORD,
because the foundation of the house of the LORD was laid. But
many of the older priests and Levites and family heads, who had
seen the former temple, wept aloud when they saw the
foundation of this temple being laid, while many others shouted
for joy. No one could distinguish the sound of the shouts of joy
from the sound of weeping, because the people made so much
noise. And the sound was heard far away." Ezra 11b-13 NIV*

The older men and priests knew that this temple would never
match up to the glory of the first. After all, King Solomon spent

a fortune on building the first temple. They also remembered the horrible end of the first temple, and these memories combined with the joy of the restoration to make profound mixed feelings in the old men.

Possibly some of them had stood on this very spot half a century before, in an agony of despair, while they saw the cruel flames licking the ancient stones and blazing up among the cedar beams, and all the fine gold dimmed with black clouds of smoke. They had seen that the glory had departed from Israel. In their circumstances it was impossible to build such a house as the first temple and had this even been possible, still it would have been greatly inferior.

There was a danger in their weeping. There are times when looking backward may have a tendency to discount the present. Regrets over the past which paralyze work in the present are always wrong. Moreover all such regrets, as in this case, are in danger of blinding the eyes to the true value and significance of the present.

But the younger people, who had no remembrance of the prior temple, felt nothing but joy in seeing this important step in the restoration of the temple. This profound scene showed the depth of the mixed feelings among the people.

The sight must have been really amazing to see--a whole people, one part crying aloud with sorrow; the other shouting aloud for joy on the same occasion-in which both sides emotional response was understandable and justified. (2006 David Guzik)

That was how I felt. Profound sorrow and joy at the same time. Jamelyn and the team were OK. They didn't mention Sr. Carmelle and Sr. Simone so we had to assume that they were OK as well and hope that was a correct assumption.

But Baby Jude and Oudel were lost.

Baby Jude...

We had met Baby Jude in November, just six weeks before the earthquake. Shelia and I had travelled to Haiti to work on a project with another organization in Jacmel. Fondwa is near Jacmel so we made a stop there for two days on our way back to the city.

It was so wonderful to see Sr. Carmelle and Sr. Simone again. It had been well over a year since we had been there. Although we kept in close contact on the phone and via email when they had access to it, we hadn't seen them in Fondwa and missed that greatly.

Sr. Carmelle was sad while we were there. Her brother, who was 48, had just died the week before of hepatitis. This kind of thing is common in Haiti. Lack of medical care for serious diseases often causes the demise of the person with the disease. She was heartbroken and had brought her 4 year old niece to Fondwa to stay with her for a while hoping she would be a source of comfort for her.

Baby Jude was a new orphan to them. He had just come to the orphanage a few months before. It was so easy to immediately fall in love with him. His sweet disposition and desire to be close to most anyone who would hold him captured my heart right away. But it was clear that he "belonged" to Sr. Carmelle. He went to others who wanted to hold him but if he had his way, he would be in her lap. We got several great photos of him and Sr. Carmelle. They are a treasure to me today.

Sr. Oudel was one of the 11 novices of their order training with Sisters Carmelle and Simone at the Sister's House in Fondwa. She was his main caregiver. She made sure he was fed and bathed and saw the he spent the time he needed napping and got him to bed when it was time. She was often seen carrying him around the guest house the two days we were there. It was a beautiful site.

Baby Jude was dead…and so was Sr. Oudel.

We were to find out later that Sr. Oudel was found on top of Jude, trying with her last breath of her too short life to protect him and save him from the terrible catastrophe that was going to consume the country of Haiti on that sunny Tuesday early in January. We were to find out later that Sr. Carmelle was in Leogane that day, a small town about 15 miles from Fondwa. She had gone to buy supplies for the mission when the earthquake hit. She felt tremendous guilt at not being there when the two of them died. She even expressed the inner thought that if she had been there she would have died trying to save them.

Shelia and I found it difficult to know how to respond. In the course of several minutes we were to find out that someone very close to us was alive, but his family was unaccounted for. We learned that the team was alive and on their way home only to find out that Jude and Oudel were now in their eternal home with the Lord.

The emotions were hard to balance.

We stopped and prayed for Sr. Carmelle and all of those in Fondwa, as well as the team. I know it must have elicited serious feelings of conflict to be evacuated at a time when that wasn't an option for many whom they knew.

I knew that Sr. Carmelle's heart was already broken when we saw her in November. A situation like this would try the faith and emotional constitution of even the strongest person. I wrote in my email update on our website later that day:

"We received a report from Fondwa. The US team that was there has been located, is safe and will be returning home in the next day or two.

Fondwa was severely hit with the earthquake. The mission guest house, which holds 40 people, was completely destroyed as was the school for 600 kids. We are assuming that Sr. Carmelle and Sr. Simone are OK since they weren't specifically mentioned. The text message did sadly report that one of the novice sisters Oudel and the 2 year old orphan that the nuns were caring for, Baby Jude, at the quest house with them died in the collapse. He was 2 years old.

To help you pray, Sr. Carmelle was in a state of near complete exhaustion when we were there in November. Her brother of 47 had just died of hepatitis the week before and she was very fragile. She had her 4 yr old niece there too. She was worried about how the family would survive now without someone who earned even a meager living. We talked to her the week before the earthquake and she was still in a severe state of worry and depression. She is the stalwart of that community and holds it together. So much on her already and now this.

Shelia and I are very worried about how this crisis will affect her already fragile psyche. Please pray for extraordinary strength to get her through this. April"

It was hard for me to understand fully how the community might be affected by the damages to the buildings as she described them. The Fondwa compound had a large three story guest house which held about 40 people, a dining area and a medical clinic. There was also a house for the novice nuns which housed about 15. It also contained a small chapel. This seemed to be where Oudel and Jude died. A few hundred yards down the road was a large school for 700 or more children. Sr. Simone was in charge of the school. Finally there was a large church which held about 200 people. This complex was the center of the community. Attached to the guest house was a newer building, Fondwa University, where 10-20 young people were studying higher education in this rural mountain village.

My heart was breaking and I was finding it more and more difficult to deal with the sense of helplessness that I was feeling here at home knowing many of my friends and people I loved were in Haiti enduring this tragedy of unknown proportions.

About noon time I got an email from the volunteer director of NC Baptist Men. He indicated that they had sent a first response scouting team earlier in the week. He was collecting contact information from those who might be able to go to Haiti but wanted the first team to evaluate what was needed before putting together the next wave of response. He indicated he had added me to the list of available people.

About mid-afternoon another email came in from him:

> *To: April Perry*
> *FYI, Today a NCBM 7 person medical team arrived in Port- au-Prince, Haiti. We have been asked to write a proposal to fill a C130 Cargo plane with people and "stuff". I need to give the authority some sort of idea of how many medical personnel can commit to go within the next 2-4 days. Details following:*
> ***Departure****: no sooner than Jan. 17*
> ***Length of stay****: approximately 7-10 days*
> ***Type of work****: provide medical help to those affected by earthquake in Haiti in primitive conditions*
> ***Lodging****: mission compound. Food, water, and a place to sleep provided*
> ***Transportation:*** *C130cargo plane*
> ***Cost:*** *very little if any*

Requirements: *must be current in your medical training and have a license to practice. MUST HAVE A   VALID PASSPORT!!!*
Health: *you need to be in good health, able to withstand long   hours in difficult conditions*
ACTION*: If you can go, reply to this email within 24 hours   with: name, profession, mobile phone number, and email.*

This proposal may be approved or disapproved by the authority. So, as we say in disaster relief work....be flexible. It could fail at any point and not come to fruition. However, many people need you in Haiti, and t his is a great opportunity if it gets approval.

Sincerely,
Gaylon Moss
Disaster Relief Director
Volunteerism Coordinator
North Carolina Baptist Men

Of course I responded back that I was available on short notice and to please add me to the "Active List".

Later in the afternoon I phoned my friend Bob Herdman in Ohio from The Hands and Feet Project (HAF) which was located in Jacmel, another area hard hit by the earthquake. We had just visited them in November and were actively partnering on planning a project with them beginning in February. Obviously that would be put on hold at this point but I wanted to see how their organization fared. As we talked I mentioned to him that we hadn't heard from Emmanuel, our translator and assistant. Emmanuel had traveled to Jacmel with us in November and Bob and he had struck up a nice friendship. I expressed my concern for him to Bob on the phone.

I was really happy when he told me that Emmanuel had sent him a message via Facebook on the day of the earthquake that he was in the Dominican Republic doing some translation work. I wanted to make sure so he checked back and said, yes. He had gotten a Facebook message that he was in the DR working. From that he assumed he was OK and out of the country-maybe trying to get back. He did indicate that he had said he had relatives who had died during the earthquake.

To know that Emmanuel was alive was such a relief and yet here was the sadness-again. We were happy Emmanuel was alive but didn't know who the relatives he was referring to were. I knew all of his brothers well.

He told me that the mission partners for our local church with HAF-Mission of Hope in Grand Goave about 30 miles from Port au Prince-where we had planned to take a mission team in September, 2010-had sustained serious damage. None of the buildings were inhabitable and the guest house, which was brand new and almost finished when we visited it last November, had been destroyed completely. He also said that our mission partner there, Lex Edme, had been in a motorcycle accident and had sustained a head injury losing consciousness and requiring treatment from the UN medical staff.

Bob told me that their orphanage at HAF had not been damaged but that Jacmel had sustained much damage. Many of the buildings there had collapsed. The mission compound was serving as a food distribution center for many people. He also said that none of their children or staff was hurt.

Knowing that Jacmel, which is about 20 miles beyond Fondwa, had sustained such damage, I was more and more concerned about the situation in Fondwa. It was like putting together a puzzle, with bits of information coming from a variety of sources and trying to see how they might all fit together to give us a picture of what things were like on the ground.

Friday night as I went to bed this was the situation as I knew it:

- Boselor Souffrant-translator and friend confirmed deceased
- Baby Jude-Fondwa-confirmed deceased
- Sr. Oudel-Fondwa confirmed deceased
- Dr. Romel--alive but unable to locate his wife Fregga and his parents
- Emmanuel-alive but lost relatives
- Lex Edme-ministry partner at Mission of Hope-survived the earthquake but was seriously injured yesterday in a motorcycle accident; he has a head injury, a severe cut to his leg and was unconscious-- being tended to by the UN. Please pray
- Pastor Jean Revil Belbede Christian church-status unknown
- Edmund Franz-medical student supported by Luke's Mission in PAP-status UNKNOWN
- Eddie Petit Homme-translator-status UNKNOWN
- Jules Remy-translator and friend-status UNKNOWN

My job of updating the website was beginning to become something that I dreaded doing.

Wall Guest House where we stayed in Port au Prince 5 deceased

Chapter 4
How are you feeling?

As Sunday came, I prepared to go to church. I am overwhelmed by my church's response to this crisis. Within 24 hours, they had supported us in doing a prayer vigil; made a list, for people desiring to do so, of "ingredients" for hygiene packs requested from the denomination. It was to be sent this week. I addressed people's desires to give donations by providing them with the needed information on reliable NGO's; met with a group who decided to divert funds from an upcoming fund raiser to Haiti.

As it happened that morning I was to be the lay scripture reader. These assignments had been made months in advance, so I began to review the reading before I went to church, wishing someone else had been assigned to lead the congregation in the scripture reading. The reading was about the miracle at the wedding at Cana. I didn't feel much like listening to a sermon about a wedding party but did the best I could to prepare.

As I entered the church one woman came up to me and quietly handed me a $100 bill, said no more and turned and walked away. I could hardly get from the foyer into the sanctuary for the people who wanted to hug me and express their concern for me and the people of Haiti. I had felt so much love and support from these dear saints of Christ since Wednesday. Many had called left messages or sent emails expressing how deeply they were concerned about our work and the people of Haiti.

As I had driven into the church parking lot, I had noticed that on the sign outside it said the title of the sermon would be "What a party". I prayed the Lord would give me something within that theme that would sooth my troubled heart.

The service was truly overwhelming. The first part progressed along as planned. I read the story of the wedding at Cana and the miracle performed there and returned to my seat. But then our pastor told us he was being obedient to the leading of the Holy Spirit and wasn't going to go along with what was printed in the bulletin. He said the sermon on the wedding at Cana just didn't seem to be what the Lord wanted him to say. He held up several pieces of paper and said he had a sermon written on this topic but he wasn't going to use it.

Then, he moved from the liturgically correct position behind the lectern and walked down the three steps from the platform into the congregation and stood among us--a move that was clearly symbolic. It was so moving to me personally, I was overcome with emotion and began to weep.

He then said, speaking to the congregation, "How are you feeling this morning? I want to know how you are feeling. It is important to me."

He allowed people to express what they were feeling as they desired while he stood among us. As he read Psalm 46 to us, he reiterated again God's desire to be our refuge among an earth that was moving and mountains that were shaking. He emphasized the phrase, "Fear not" and again helped us know that we have no reason to be afraid. He assured us that God is in control and that the Haitian people are in His hands.

As we closed with the old, old hymn, A Mighty Fortress is our God-again veering from the program-I found myself overwhelmed as I read the words ".....a bulwark never failing."

I usually go to Sunday school but that particular morning, I was too emotionally exhausted from the service I had just attended to do anything else. I decided to just go home and try to collect myself after such a powerful experience.

The outpouring of assistance and support from those around me was incredible. I was to learn later that my Sunday school class took up a spontaneous offering for Luke's Mission to provide earthquake relief to the people we minister to. In that spontaneous offering, the final tally came to $962! One woman even indicated that she didn't have her check book with her and put an IOU in the offering basket.

When I got home, I had a message on the machine informing me that a Seniors SS class at a local church had collected $84 in cash and wanted to give 2 water filters through the matching donation program from our water filters vendor so that they could now give 4. Another friend called me to tell me that the CNA who cares for her elderly parents had given her $80 in cash that she wanted to go to help Haiti.

My hair stylist called. She wanted to know how they could help. After talking with her about some options she decided that two of her stylists would give free cuts for the next 10 days for a $25 donation and contribute the money for our relief efforts-Haircuts for Haiti. I was truly overwhelmed. Eventually their efforts led to collecting $450 for water filters for the relief efforts.

I decided to put some thoughts on the website blog. This was the entry on Sunday January 16. The newspaper read it and published it as an op-ed piece on Monday.

> *"As I write this, I am drinking coffee that I purchased at the Caribbean Market in Haiti only 7 weeks ago. I saw pictures of the Caribbean Market on CNN last night completely destroyed as a search and rescue team was still trying to get someone they thought was alive out of the rubble. I saw yesterday a reporter who said Leogane is 90% destroyed with 4300 already dead in a mass grave. That thought sickens me. We have been there many times. These kinds of things prevent me from watching the TV too much. We know these places, we*

know these people.

What am I feeling my pastor asked yesterday? The best I can say is overwhelmed--on many levels.

We met with our Haiti Mission team tonight for our regularly scheduled team meeting. We showed them pictures of the BEFORE and AFTER of Mission of Hope where we will travel in September. It was eerie that I had taken nearly identical views as Renee-our mission partner- did in some of her pictures sent to us after the earthquake. None of their buildings are useable and everything in their compound and home will need to be rebuilt.

I found myself overwhelmed as I tried helped this team of people try their best to get an understanding of a situation that I-someone who understands Haiti very well-cannot even begin to grasp. I remember on Wednesday morning someone asking me what the impact of this would be and my response even then was-I cannot imagine in my mind how this would play itself out. I wasn't just talking about the devastation, but what would this do to the future of Haiti. To rebuild an area the size of the Triangle here in NC from ground zero is an undertaking that is enormous-even here with all of the resources and a functional government. I couldn't then and still can't now imagine how this will happen in Haiti--and how long it will take.
As I entered church yesterday, I knew that my many Haitian friends were also assembled in worship--I have no doubt of it. And that in the midst of this terrible catastrophe, they also were praising God for his strength and power. I know them and I know this was occurring. I was deeply comforted by that.

I covet your prayers for them as we go forward to see

*what further difficulties we will need to face together
and how the Lord will use us to build His kingdom
through that.*

*I will leave you with a comment that broke my heart.
When Shelia talked to our friend from Haiti Sonel last
night, one of the final things he said to her was "Please
don't forget us". The Haitian people have been through
this before--people giving help at a crisis and then
leaving them to make it yet again on their own. Shelia
assured him that we at Luke's Mission are with them for
the long haul and they could count on   that and that
Haiti was front and center in all of the news media
and they are not forgotten--at least for now.
Under His crushing mercy,
April"*

The sense of helplessness was growing increasingly harder for
me to deal with. I prayed that God would provide a way for me
to go to Haiti. Even if I was little or no help, just being I felt my
presence there might bring some measure of comfort that these
beloved people were indeed, not forgotten.

Monday morning came and I had my morning coffee again from
the Caribbean Market. I had errands to run. Upon returning I
checked my email again and found two wonderful messages.

The first was from Romel. Romel and his wife Fregga and his
parents are safe. He said he had seen them briefly and knew they
were OK. I praised the Lord for that. He still could not make
contact with Pastor Jean Revil. Jean is Romel's best friend so he
has been trying very hard to find him. Additionally we still
hadn't heard from our translator/friend Jules.

The next one was the one I had been waiting for:
*Date: Mon, 18 Jan 2010 13:22:11 -0500
From: NC Baptist Men's Disaster Relief*

To: April Perry
April,
The plan is to depart tomorrow Jan. 19 at 12:35 p.m.
and return Jan. 28. No charge for airfare or logistics.
Can you go?
Gaylon

Immediately I sent the following email:

"Gaylon:
YES!!! Call me if I need to do any more
April"

I was ecstatic. God had given me the desire of my heart. I was going to get to go to Haiti!

Immediately I sent the following email out to our distribution list (those who had contacted us and said they were interested in keeping up with the news as we received it;-the list consisted of several hundred names)

"I got the call to go to Haiti.
I am leaving with the NC Baptist Relief tomorrow at
12:35   p.m. and returnJan.28.
Details to follow. Please add me to your prays as I
minister to my beloved Haitian people
Under His crushing mercy
April"

I thought I might have an idea of what it might mean to be ready "at a moment's notice" which is what I was told last week when this plan was first presented to me. But now I had less than 18 hrs to get ready. Even though I did all my laundry last week and had a packing list in my head, it was really hard to mobilize myself for this. That part ended up being more challenging than I anticipated.

Along with the packing list in my head, there were so many last minute things that I needed to do. It took a while to get things into place. From the moment I thought I might get to go to Haiti to do relief work, I felt an intense desire to try to bring the story back to people here. I had some sort of idea what might be happening there because of my previous history of working in Haiti. I just didn't think that people here had a real understanding of the tremendous impact this kind of disaster would have in a third world country.

It was Martin Luther King Day when I received the call so both Shelia and I had the day off. I immediately called my supervisor and left a message for her to call me immediately when she was available. I phoned my colleague at work who had offered to cover for me and told her what had happened. I would go through my calendar and come up with a list of things that we needed to talk about later in the day.

I wanted to get a phone that would allow me to communicate back here from Haiti-hopefully that would allow email. So Shelia and went to the phone store and spent two precious hours purchasing a Blackberry which would allow both international phone calls and unlimited email access. It was guaranteed to work from Haiti even with little cell phone service. It cost more than what we had budgeted but the sense of urgency I felt about keeping in touch with information to those Stateside remained a priority. These things took most of the afternoon and I had yet to even pull out the suitcase.

Only the week before, we had gotten a call from a nurse colleague who had a large donation of supplies from a quadriplegic patient who had died. He left 23 large boxes of medical supplies that she asked if we could use for our medical mission trip. Fortunately, the week before, I had sorted through each of boxes which were stored in my garage, putting all of the same supplies together in some semblance of order. I knew exactly now what would be useful in Haiti for this disaster.

As soon as we got home from the phone store, Shelia and I began going through the boxes and putting the dressing materials, tape, and other medical supplies that I knew would be useful into the canvas bags that we take to Haiti on our medical mission trips. We packed two of them full, with what we thought might be 50 pounds-the allotted weight limit for the international flight to the Dominican Republic. It was now nearly 7:00 PM.

I realized that the overnighted shipment of water filters had not come in. I phoned the Fed-Ex company and they indicated that since we had not been home the driver had not left them because he needed a signature. We had left a note on the garage for him but apparently he had not seen it. So with everything else I had to do, I had 90 minutes to get to the Fed-Ex office in the Research Triangle Park-about 30 miles from my house-to pick up the package before they closed for the evening.

Shelia and I jumped in the car and headed to the RTP to try to get those filters before they closed. We printed out the directions to the office but got hopelessly lost. It was an area we weren't at all familiar with and we made a wrong turn. Where was the GPS when you needed it? Fortunately we saw a Fed-Ex/Kinkos store and stopped there. He had pre-printed directions to the store. We got there just 10 minutes before they closed. We retrieved the box with the 50 filters in it and headed home. It was now nearly 9:00 PM and I hadn't even started to pack my own things.

We stuffed the water filters into the two canvas bags and I began to do my own packing. Since I was taking supplies in my allotment of checked baggage, that left me a carry on to put my own things in. I am accustomed to this as this is usually the procedure the mission team uses to pack. But it still takes a lot more time to pack that little suitcase because every single item has to be evaluated as to its need, how to best fold/put it in the suitcase to maximize in the space. I often tell my team members to think about what you "need" and not about what you "want".

But it still takes a lot of time. Additionally in packing for Haiti, one has to pack things like bug spray, mosquito net, flip flops, towels and this time we were instructed to bring our own sheets.

At 11:30, I gave up; I was really tired and just couldn't do any more. I vowed to set the alarm early and get up to finish. 5:30 the next morning came all too soon.

I went through my calendar and sent an email to my colleague telling her I would have a couple of hours at the airport to wait and would call her from there to discuss the work coverage. That seemed to be the best use of my time. I wanted to get some final thoughts down on paper (or the screen) so I began to write a letter to those interested about what was going on, give them some information and let them know how they could pray.

Before I could write anything, I noticed an email from Romel. He said that he had been able to locate his wife and parents and they were all safe. That was a matter for praise! We still had not been able to make contact with Pastor Jean Revil and Romel had not been able to either. Jean is Romel's best friend so he had been trying very hard to find him. Additionally we still hadn't heard from our translator/friend, Jules. So I updated our website with this new information.

I had spoken with both Romel and Emmanuel last night on the phone. Both had called me when they read my email that I was coming to Haiti. They knew my schedule and we planned to hook up on Thursday. I felt like I would be so grateful to give both of them big hugs and know that they were truly OK.

The plan was for us to fly to Santa Domingo DR that day where we would stay overnight and travel to PAP tomorrow morning early via bus. There were still no commercial flights to Port au Prince and none expected for the foreseeable future. Since the C130 cargo plane proposal wasn't accepted, the volunteer coordinator decided to go forward with commercial flights to the

DR and travel. That was how most of the press had been getting into Haiti.

I was to be traveling with the NC Baptist Men Relief Organization, a well known, well organized disaster and relief group. These people are professionals and have travelled all over the world doing disaster relief. In fact the Southern Baptist has one of the best organized groups doing relief in the country. In the early 90's the Southern Baptist convention had a mandate to make disaster relief one of their priorities and they have honed it down to a science. I experienced this when we worked in Katrina side by side with them, which was why I originally signed up with them to be of assistance in these kinds of situations.

I hoped that people wouldn't think I was going off with some half-baked group. At that point, as much as I wanted to go to Haiti, I would only go under an umbrella aid organization. Those who had seen how I worked with our mission teams knew that safety is a priority for me and I apply that to myself as well my teams.

As tempting as it would have been to just high-tail it to Haiti as soon as I could, the lack of on-the-ground contacts, a place to stay, access to water and food all would have made that a very foolish decision. Foods, logistics, lodging were all difficult to obtain and one needed to have someone who had contacts to make sure that these details were cared for. I felt confident that they had the resources to put these things in place for us and wanted those at home to as well.

Shelia and I had talked about the risk involved in traveling to Haiti the evening before. We both agreed, with our knowledge of Haiti and all we could discern about the situation on the ground now, that this trip will be no more risky than any other trip we have made there and maybe less at this time because of the increased military presence on the ground now and the over arching concern for safety among relief workers.

So I prayed and, as I told my mom last week, I told the Lord it was the desire of my heart to be there if at all possible, and could He grant this desire for me. He did.

Our mission was to provide medical care to people affected by the Haitian earthquake the week before. The current scenario was post-op care in the Petionville Community Hospital. We would be staying at the Global Outreach –Haiti compound in Titiyen. I knew this area well, having travelled to this specific location in November with Shelia. They have a small burn clinic there. It was possible we might be of use there as well.

We were a 10 person team. I gave people their names and asked them to pray for them individually. They came from all areas of the state-Charlotte, Winston-Salem, Fayetteville, several from Raleigh-Durham, and other parts of the state. We were going to all meet in Miami, leaving NC from two airports. We were to be joined in the DR by 2 physicians from Hungary, working also with the international arm of the Baptist Men. I spoke with the team leader the night before concerning some last minute questions. He was also grateful for my experience in Haiti as I was the only person on the team who had actually worked in Haiti.

In talking to Romel the evening before, he said the hospital in the area where he is (called Les Cayes or Cayes), which was about 30 miles from Port au Prince, had many earthquake victims coming there for treatment but there has been no assistance received for them. Even as he was talking to me an ambulance was driving up with several from PAP in it. I hoped we could provide some help to them. While I was grateful for all of the love and support that people had been showing me, I was overwhelmed with the emails. While I wanted to answer all of them, I sent a mass email explaining that I just couldn't but I assured them that I had read each and every one.

I was taking 70 water filters donated by friends of Luke's Mission. Emmanuel had agreed to assist me in seeing that these got into the hands of those who needed them now and in the coming days.

I felt as prepared as I could be for what lay ahead. As I had watched the TV coverage I noticed aid workers and reporters being shocked by things like lack of electricity, difficult roads and the poverty. I wouldn't be shocked by these things. This is a baseline for our many trips to Haiti previously. So I hoped that I would be one step ahead of that.

I saw the tremendous devastation only 5 days after Katrina-things looked like an explosion had gone off-so I had some experience with that. I would be putting the two of those situations together. I knew the impact of knowing this had happened to people I know and love would be the most difficult part—or so I thought. But, I really wondered if one could truly prepare one's self for these kinds of things? I just didn't know.

What I did know was that I would feel better experiencing those feelings in the presence of my Haitian friends than I would here...from the TV. Being there will be a "blessed burden"-a real paradox but I am sure you know what I mean. If I can even offer a cup of water or a hand to hold, it will be worth it all. And just to physically see my beloved friends and colleagues there will be a blessing I felt I would find it difficult to be able to describe.

In my departing email, posted at 5:56 AM--I asked people if they would pray for Shelia as she held down the fort here. We had several speaking engagements and other commitments that week related to this crisis that she was going to have to manage by herself. We sat down the night before and went over everything that needed to be done and got things in order for that.

Additionally, I knew her heart wanted so badly to be there as well. It must have been a terrible feeling for her. But she was the stalwart of support for me despite her own feelings.

I thanked the church who had donated some left over supplies from a mission program that had disbanded. They had been sitting in our garage since last fall—and now would be on their way to Haiti to help in this disaster. I wanted people to know that I was taking some cash with me from the donations that have been given to Luke's Mission to use for those affiliated with Luke's Mission as I saw the needs there.

I explained that Shelia would be my main contact and that she would forward any information from either my email or her own. I hoped people would look for updates that way. I had also sent out an email call for someone who could update our website while I was away. My dear friend, Carol Ann volunteered as she had website experience. So I quickly sent her the access information and a quick update on how to post on the blog section. She was a lifesaver.

My supervisor at Duke HomeCare and Hospice had been so supportive. My boss said "Just go--Just go" without a second thought. She knew the impact that my Haiti work had on me and had been right there with me when I had been awarded the Community Caregiver of the Year award less than a week before. I was also so grateful to my colleague Carol Ann Mullis for stepping up and covering for me while I was away on such short notice—(incidentally, she is the one who nominated me for the award).

Several people had mentioned the way I had been closing me emails "Under His crushing mercy". I told them the story of my friend Karen and her insight about the paradoxical feelings with regards to the award and the earthquake. I explained that I had been comforted by that knowing that I am under His crushing mercy.

I also shared that Karen had written me something the night before that has brought me great comfort as I think of the deaths of our three friends, Bosie, Sr. Oudel and baby Jude.

"I looked at the photos you sent this weekend with heavy heart,   even as I thanked God for His mercy that would   bring so many   into His heaven in one flashing moment
Karen."

"…So many brought into His eternal presence in one flashing moment…" I was greatly comforted in knowing it was in "one flashing moment" and not longer.

God had been good. His mercy had endured and would endure forever. As this next part of our journey would begin, I, along with the Haitian people, were finding ourselves just now...under His crushing mercy.

Team prayer before leaving Dominican Republic for Haiti

Chapter 5
Ground Zero

Our trip to Haiti was a long, convoluted and complex one. Some of us met at Raleigh Durham airport to link up with the rest of the team in Charlotte. From there, we would travel to Santa Domingo, Dominican Republic. We would meet up there with a group of 4 Hungarian physicians and EMT's who also worked with Baptist Men in Hungary.

We arrived in DR about 9:30 in the evening. It took several hours to sort out exactly what we would be doing, where we would be going, and get our papers in order. We were to stay with a local pastor and his family for the night and then take a bus from DR to Haiti the next day.

The facilities were at a local seminary. The three women stayed in the local pastors home in his daughters room. It was comfortable. We had beds, water and food. That was all I really needed.

The next day we began what turned out to be the 12 hour bus ride through the DR to the Haitian border. Because so many relief workers were accessing Haiti through the DR, the border crossing proved to be even more complex and took three house to go through.

Shortly after arriving in Haiti proper, we got the proverbial flat tire-which is a main stay when traveling the pot hole infested roads that make up the infrastructure of the country. After changing the tire, we had to take additional time getting the tire fixed in a small village so we wouldn't be left without a spare.

When we got to the outskirts of Port au Prince, I began to recognize where I was. However, it was now dusk and driving in Haiti after dark brings with it its own problems. Our Dominican driver wasn't really sure of where we were to go. We were in the Croix de Bouquet area which I was very familiar with. Fortunately we had picked up a missionary couple who would be helping out at the guest facilities we were to be staying at and they knew where to go. However, it was completely dark by the time we got on the road leading out of Port au Prince to Titiyen, where we were to stay.

We were staying at the Global Outreach compound. It was a large compound. The dorms were co-ed and large with about 75 sets of bunk beds in each of the two dorms we were using. When we arrived, they were expecting us. We had a quick supper and then planned a meeting with the Baptist Men team that was already there. They briefed us on the situation, the system they had set up to work in the hospitals and gave us the information we needed to begin our tour. Our plan was to leave early the next day as they indicated it had taken them 2 hours to make what normally would be a 45 minute trip due to the traffic, food distribution lines and other post earthquake problems.

I awoke early the morning of our first day of relief work. It was a gorgeous day in Haiti-bright and beautiful like most of them start out. Days in Haiti start with the sunrise. Because most people have little, if any access to electricity, the days are marked by the rising and setting of the sun. Work starts at sunrise and bedtime comes at dusk. Our days were no different.

It was the first time we had been able to see the whole Global Outreach Haiti compound. It was lovely. The compound sprawled over 60 acres, we were to learn later. The dorm building we were staying in was located near the back of the property so that our view looked over the entire complex. The missionaries' there-8 all toll-provided this as a conference center of sorts for Haitian pastors. They hosted continuing education and church building seminars for the most part. The compound was very well equipped. We had seen the lights welcoming us the evening before. They went all the way up the half mile long drive from the main road to the compound entrance. That is a luxury in Haiti-generator power to operate lights like this after dark. Right next to our co-ed dorm was a large open are tabernacle. This reminded me of the camp meetings of my childhood, where we had week long revivals at the denomination camp ground. It was a very large structure comprised of just a roof-all four wall areas were completely open air. There was a large stage area with a podium. Simple benches provided eating for about 300 people.

Several other dorm buildings speckled the beautiful "oasis in the desert" mission. Along with them, one saw the generator house, a very large porch type meeting area, the shower building and of course the preverbal latrine house. The mission was landscaped beautifully with native plants and bushes, all topical plants native to Haiti but which gave it a very soothing look as one looked over the acreage from the dorm.

We were joined at the mission compound by a group from Samaritan's Purse. Samaritan's Purse was on the ground less than 24 hours after the earthquake. Their medical relief work was based at Baptist Haiti Mission in Kenskoff. Kenskoff is located on the outskirts of Port au Prince, about 10 miles up a winding mountain road which takes about an hour to traverse. Baptist Haiti Mission is a place well known to me. I have visited the mission many times while in Haiti. Three generations of Turnbull's had been the mainstay of the Baptist Haiti Mission for nearly 50 years. It seems like their family tree has its roots now in Haiti. Their work was marked by a mission compound which housed a large hospital, church, arts and craft store known as "Mountain Maid as well as a small restaurant. We always love to take the teams up to BHM near the end of the week because they have hamburgers and sub sandwiches like we get her in the

US. It is always a great joy to have food like we eat at home and everyone enjoys it.

This group with Samaritan's Purse, though was working on long term strategic planning and logistics. They were about 80 in number.

Breakfast was in the mess hall. The hall held about 250 people. Tables were arranged in long rows. A simple yet functional set up-this is how many things are in Haiti. Breakfast was composed of numerous boxes of cereal, pitchers of milk, and a large pot of oatmeal accompanied by bananas, peanut butter and Haitian rolls. I have found that this is a typical breakfast served to us on mission trips. Again, simple yet functional.

As we ate our breakfast, we all had a sense of excitement tempered with a reasonable degree of anticipation and anxiety. We were final going to be able to do what we had been sent here to do and were ready to get about the task.

From what I could discern based upon Team 1's description of the choices of work places, I had decided that because I know the health care system in Haiti and had some sense of what might lay ahead as far as facilities, I would be best used at Petionville Hospital doing triage with the physicians there. We had been told that the traffic was making things very difficult for the previous team-taking nearly two hours to get to the location. As a result, our team decided we would be ready to leave at 7 AM hoping to be able to get a long day in for our first one.

We were all assembled at the pickup point for the bus only to have multiple things delay us-again something that often happens in Haiti as well as in disaster situations. Things rarely go as planned and flexibility is needed to handle the situation. Several others wanted to join our group-several from our group wanted to ride with another group. After about 20 minutes, we were all on our respective buses and began the trip to Port au Prince.

As we drove out the gate down the mile long drive way to the Global Outreach Compound, our leader asked that we stop and asked the Lord to bless our work that day.

Driving down the main road from Titiyen (pronounced Tee-tie-yen) we drove by two notable things. The first is the "rotten egg waters". The road goes right along the edge of the northern coast of the southern peninsula of Haiti. Much raw sewage and garbage are dumped into the sea waters off the coast of Haiti. In this particular area, decay of this organic matter along with chemical reactions with the sulfur-containing minerals in soil and rock to produce hydrogen sulfide gas along the coast in this area. The hydrogen sulfide gas has an odor which mimics the smell of rotten eggs that permeates this area.

The smell is very strong. It is rare that anyone can really tolerate it at all and most people have to cover their noses and/or breathe through their mouths for the mile or so through the area affected. This was no different for our team.

The second notable area in Titiyen was equally as obnoxious only in a different way. During the reign of Papa Doc Duvalier, the infamous dictator who ruled Haiti for 30 years in the mid twentieth century, the Haitian police force was equally infamous for their corruption and torture tactics used to keep the peace. They were known as the Tonton macoutes- which translates as "Uncle Gunnysack". This name originated from Haitian Creole mythology. It was the name of a bogeyman that walked the streets after dark, and would kidnap children who stayed out too late. He stowed them away in his gunnysack, never to be seen again.

Duvalier employed the Tonton Macoutes in a reign of terror against any opponents, including those who proposed

75

progressive social systems. Those who spoke out against Duvalier would disappear at night, or were sometimes attacked in broad daylight. They were never seen again. They were believed to have been abducted and killed by the *Tonton Macoutes*. Anyone who challenged the Tonton Macoutes risked assassination. Their unrestrained terrorism was accompanied by corruption, extortion and personal aggrandizement among the leadership.

It is well documented that the location of many of these bodies were mass graves in this area of Titiyen. In the 1990's, human rights workers came to the area and unearthed many mass graves containing bodies of people executed by the Tonton Macoutes as a record for all of history of the atrocities that had been committed against innocent Haitians by this tyrannical dictatorship.

This area is marked by large deposits of minerals and white rock. Many quarry-like areas can be observed along this stretch of road-quarries from which much of the concrete was made that was used to build the structures that now lay in ruins all over the city.

We were to also find out that the mass graves from the earthquake were also located on this stretch of road. The first time we passed the area where the earthquake mass graves were, the driver quietly pointed out to us that this is where many people were buried who died as a result of the tragedy. We all silently looked at the area he pointed out to us outside the left hand bus window.

We observed a large area at the bottom of the stone quarry with several bull dozer type machines were sitting. It was clear that the earth had recently been disturbed. Although we had passed through the "rotten egg water" area, the smell of death clearly permeated this area. The media had reported that thousands of people had been buried in mass graves in an effort to prevent disease and to remove the dead quickly. The grisly but necessary job of burying thousands of people lay with the men who would run these machines later in the day. I would see why this was needed in a more personal way later in the week.

Obviously, none of the dead were identified before burial. No records were kept of those in these massive human tombs. Families would just know that their loved one had died and somehow had been disposed of when they could not find them or they didn't show up back at home sometime after the earth quake. This was just one more deeply disturbing part of this whole inhuman situation.

How ironic that the mass graves now being used to dispose of the earthquake victims were also located on this stretch of road as well.

Our driver, Jude, was employed by the mission. He was more of the kind of Haitian driver that I am used to as opposed to the Dominican driver. We were all concerned about the report of taking 2 hours to get to the hospital. But Jude drove us really fast down the stretch of road where there was no traffic. Once into the city he continued to drive faster but carefully.

As we approached the Croix de Bouquet-the extremely congested area we had come through the evening before, we got our first visions of some of the damage. Although we would see an occasional building collapsed, most only had large cracks in them or a missing wall—and these were sporadic. I allowed myself to be deluded into thinking that this might not be as bad as I thought.

Additionally, I noticed the streets. This seemed to be no different than what I might see on another day in Haiti. I was thinking that the streets would be deserted, no one out and about. I am not sure where I thought they would be but I will admit that seeing normal sidewalk traffic and people was surprising to me.

The closer we got to the city, the more damage we saw. But the people on the streets only changed in that there were more of them. Some of the street vendors were open, as I might be used to seeing. We pulled onto Delmas (pronounced Dell-ma), the main street of the capital city. Delmas is the reference point for all of the other streets in this center of Port au Prince. Each side street was named Delmas and then a number indicating its location on the main Delmas. For example, the guest house we usually stayed at was Walls Guest house located on Delmas 19- the nineteenth street off of Delmas heading north.

I begin to see more damage on Delmas. A number of buildings were completely in ruins. We saw more than one two story building that had collapsed-only the roof and floors remaining-everything in between in ruins. It looked like a concrete sandwich.

I know Delmas well-having travelled it many times to various destinations while travelling in Haiti. But because of the damage, landmarks that might assist me in marking my location were unrecognizable. I was disoriented as to where we were. I knew that the Caribbean market had sustained severe damage. So I asked Jude to point out the Caribbean Market to me when we got near it.

Again, the streets were lined with people-a normal scene to me in Haiti. Although there were clear signs of damage, it didn't seem at that point as wide spread as what the news reports had indicated. Although I didn't share this with my team mates, I thought that perhaps the areas of damage were localized and less extensive than what might have been shown on TV. That gave me a sense of hope-which turned out to be a false hope.

After about 10 minutes of travel up Delmas, through normally congested traffic, Jude turned his head to me and said "There is the Market".

I looked out the left hand side window and gasped at what I saw. The three story building was now reduced to a pile of rubble about 6 feet high-less than the height of one story. The gate was bolted shut but it was clear just how much damage was sustained.

The earthquake happened at 4:10 PM. The Caribbean Market would have been full at that time of day-many people purchasing things for the evening meal. This was the first time I realized the impact of the news reports of people trapped in the collapsed buildings.

The smell of decomposing bodies was strong and overwhelming to myself as well as wall of my team mates- a couple of whom, in a moment of insensitivity and perhaps emotional immaturity, shouted to Jude "Hurry up and get by this place. It smells really bad."

We were there 7 days after the earthquake. Bodies were still trapped in that rubble-if the odor was a telling sign, it was likely many. There had been little done to try to recover them because of the weight of the rubble. It would be impossible to move without large machinery-nonexistent in Haiti.

Any bit of hope I had at that point that this would not be as bad as I might have imagined it, went out the open window as the smell of death entered it. I realized now that this was indeed going to be worse than what was possible for me to imagine.

We entered Petionville turning on Delmas 39. Petionville is knows as a place in the city where the rich live. It doesn't look like a wealthy community. Nothing does in Haiti. Wealth and all that accompanies it, in Haiti is strewn among the poor in a sporadic manner. A wealthy person would, as likely as not, live near a group of shanties-the wealthy home would just have a stone wall with glass embedded in concrete on the top to protect them from intruders while living next door to those living in

79

abject poverty.   However, more wealthy people lived in Petionville than many other areas of the city.

At the first news of the earthquake in the US, they reporters noted that a hospital had collapsed in Petionville. This was a smaller hospital that served the poor. It did collapse and most in it perished.   So our team had Petionville as a reference point due to previous news reports.

We finally rounded the corner and saw the sign for "HCH-Haitienne   Communite   Hopital-(translated   Petionville Community Hospital) -the place where our team was to be deployed for tour time of service. The sign itself was interesting. On the top of it were three black health care professional dressed in scrubs like what one might see in any US hospital, smiling, looking happy in their work, while standing behind a very nice counter top- apparently depicting an area of patient care in the hospital.   This was nothing like anything I had seen while visiting Haitian hospitals but maybe this hospital, which I was not familiar with would be different.

Maybe, just maybe, we would have at least some resources to do what we needed to do. Maybe, just maybe, this one would be different.

Devastation in downtown Port au Prince, January 12, 2010

Chapter 6
Petionville Community Hospital

None of us were prepared for what awaited us as we rounded the final corner of the pot hole ridden driveway to the hospital. At first my eyes couldn't really believe what I was seeing.

Both sides of the driveway seemed to be littered with white and colored speckles which made no earthly sense. In some ways it looked like confetti-some white, some bright blue and white striped, some other colors- strewn across the small lawn area around the driveway. But as I came to understand exactly what we were seeing it reminded me of something else I had once seen- something quite eerie. I was reminded of the millions of pieces of paper that laid on yet another ground zero-that of the Twin Towers after the terrorist attack of 9/11. In my mind's eye I saw the millions upon millions of pieces of paper floating through the air and coming to land on the ground—a symbol of the massive destruction that had taken place. This scene also symbolized that same kind of destruction.

What we were seeing were the first of many small communities composed of these sheet shelters. They weren't tents really. They were literally a bed sheet strung up on 4 poles no bigger than my arm. Under the sheet covering were one, two, or more patients. As we passed by the first few I realized that these were makeshift "patient rooms". I saw people in these shelters who were seriously ill-I could see that from the bus. Many had broken limbs, the sun reflecting brightly on the shining steel that indicated an external fixator was present on their broken extremity. External fixator is used to stabilize broken bones without casting and provide a superior result to traditional "setting" of fractures. But these were not available in Haiti on a normal day. Clearly they had been shipped in after the disaster.

Patients lay on a variety of things under these sheet protectors. Some had old and rusty but functional hospital beds. Others had make shift cots made out of an old air mattress or a small bed. Most were just lying on large pieces of cardboard, the size of a large box, which had been flattened and provided protection from the ground itself. There was an occasional pup type tent, but most were under the sheet shelters.

As we continued around the quarter mile traffic circle to the hospital entrance, the sheet shelters multiplied. It was clear there were hundreds of patients in these "patient rooms". At this point, I began to wonder what the inside of the hospital was like. We pulled up to the front of this hospital. It was a small hospital but typical for Haiti. Haitian hospitals are usually laid out in a large square with rooms around the outside surrounding a central open air court yard. Since air conditioning is not something found routinely anywhere in Haiti, this was a typical tropical architectural style to allow for the most ventilation during the hot days. This one was no different.

We entered the front door, passing by yet more of the patients whose care was being given outside on the lawns. Inside was a scene which we had been prepared for. As I have said before, it is rare that I have been in a Haitian hospital where I had not seen at least a few patients lying on the floors in some places. But, just like Bryce had said the night before, patients were EVERYWHERE. There was little floor space which was not taken up by someone. Here, as outside, most were lying on pieces of cardboard or a small blanket to protect them from the hard concrete floor.

Immediately upon entering, we were introduced to Yvonne, a white woman with an English accent. She was running here and there and stopped briefly when she saw the new team from the

Baptist Men or the "red shirts" as we came to become fondly known.

She told us she would give us a tour but to just give her a moment. When she returned, she began to describe the situation to us. Where we were standing was the triage area. There weren't many acute patients yet but it was early in the day and the line had already begun forming outside as we walked in. Here patients would be seen by someone and a decision would be made as to the level of care they needed. Following triage evaluation, they would be seen in one of the four "zones" which were located in the open air courtyard immediately inside the front door, centrally located surrounded by the rest of the hospital. Several patients were already in this area, having come in the day before.

She took us down a small hallway and into a small room on the right. This was the "post op" ward, she explained. I was accustomed to seeing this in Haitian hospitals but my teammates were all shocked. A room the size of my living room at home had about 15 patients in it. Two had beds. One father and son, both injured, shared a bed. The others were lying on the ground mostly on cardboard, a couple had thin mattresses. A centrally located desk was where the supplies needed to care for these patients were located. The room was so crowded that no more than two additional people could enter and still have room to walk around. All were injured but no one appeared to be seriously injured or like they were going to succumb from their injuries. All were alert and talking. Few looked like they were in pain. There was no nurse or any other kind of health care provider around.

I knew this was a normal situation in Haitian hospitals. It usually wasn't this crowded but I had seen an emergency room similar to this. However, as we continued down the hall and saw several other rooms with the exact same situation, I began to realize the enormity of the situation here. We went into, at least, three other "post-op wards" just like this one. We then entered into a large area in the back of the hospital, which led to the operating room suite. This large area again was filled to the brim with patients, most who had dressings or casts on, indicating they had had surgery for a broken bone or a serious wound. Family members crowded into the rooms to assist in their care, leaning forward as a new group of relief workers came around hoping they could do something different to make their situation better.

The operating room suite was a new part of the hospital. There was a sign indicating the donor who had paid for this new area. There were two fully functional operating rooms, similar to what we have in the States, but a scaled down version. I noticed they were all air conditioned. On one of the OR room doors were two pieces of 2 inch white tape. The top one said "OR 2". Carefully placed under it was a second piece of white tape which said "Swedish Team". These signs told which group of relief workers was in charge of this OR. In the pre-op area we had to carefully step over many patients lying on the floor waiting for their turn for surgery.

As we passed through the OR area, Yvonne took us to the last room in that suite. They had taken one of the OR's and made it into an Intensive Care unit of sorts. Here, in this air conditioned unit, were patients who needed closer attention than those in the post op areas or hallways, and they were monitored by one nurse constantly. There were spaces for 10 patients around the outside of the room with a desk centrally located serving as a nurse's station and supply depot.

There were no doctors assigned to this area. One nurse from another relief team was there. She explained that when she needed something she just went out and grabbed whoever was available to help her or help make care decisions.

As our "tour" ended, Yvonne called out as she exited down the hall back to the triage area, "That is your choice. Now where do you want to work?"

And off she went.

We all just stood there immobilized. Finally, Eric, a physician from the first team who was staying behind to help get us started, told us that maybe we should probably just continue on with running the triage today since that was the system they had established and then we could regroup in the evening and see what people thought.

He quickly went through the system they had established. Most of the people on the first team were paramedics so the system they put in place was a disaster model that many emergency workers use.

He explained that people would come in to the triage staging center in the front lobby. He would quickly determine what their level of care need was. There were 3 categories-OR 1-needing surgery today-urgent; OR-2-need surgery tomorrow or the next day; they were stable and surgery was needed but could wait; 3-TBS-to be seen-non urgent need but could wait until more other urgent needs were taken care of.

Once the level of care needed was determined, he would place a small piece of tape on their forehead with the code-OR1, OR2 or TBS-that indicated their level of need. They would then be directed to a holding/waiting area and someone there who was handling the patient flow would put them in to see the next provider in the triage zone who was available.

The courtyard was divided up into 4 "zones"-another component of a disaster model of giving medical care. Each zone encompassed one quarter of the courtyard. A zone had a health care provider-a nurse practitioner, physician assistant or physician-who would see the patient, evaluate them medically and then decide what needed to be done from that point on. Did they need x-rays, dressing, or some other kind of treatment? Most needed some form of x-ray. We were told to expect many fractures.

The hospital was equipped with a single x-ray machine. There was no CT scanner and certainly no MRI. In all of Haiti there isn't an MRI. I think I know of only one CT scanner. There was one Haitian technician working in the x-ray room at HCH.

Eric took his place at the front entrance and began seeing the patients who were already lined up outside. Several of our paramedics decided to make rounds on the people in the sheet city outside and see what they needed. The two physicians and I took our places in one of the four zones. I was in Zone 4 located directly next to the triage area.

In my zone, there were two chairs. Next to the chairs was a small cardboard box. It contained several boxes of gloves, some bandages, tape and a few rolls of gauze. Also in the box were a couple of IV bags and some IV tubing. Nothing was very organized. We had been shown a small supply room across from the court yard where we could look for things we needed and were also advised that the main supply depot was upstairs. If we needed anything we should go up there.

Eric sent me my first patient. He was a young man maybe in his late teens. His left arm had been amputated high above his elbow. He looked weak as he walked to the chair and sat down. His stump had a dressing on it but it was soiled and needed changing. Since there were no medical charts to use, the relief workers told each patient they had to be responsible for keeping their papers and x-rays with them. This system worked remarkably well considering the chaos around us.

I took his papers and through my translator asked him what brought him here today. He told us he was supposed to come back today to get his dressing changed and to get "this". He handed me a small vial. The vial contained a single dose of tetanus. I quickly looked over the papers. He had sustained a serious injury in the earthquake and the development of gangrene had necessitated that his arm be amputated.

He looked like he was in pain so I asked him "Eske ou fe mal?" Are you in pain?

He nodded his head yes. I thought before I attempted to change this dressing, I needed to make sure he had some pain medication on board. I asked him if he was taking any medications. He pulled out a worn out envelope, the small kind that one uses to mail a check or bill in. Inside were the remaining doses of a prescription for doxycycline-an antibiotic. Doxycycline is not the drug of choice for post operative antibiotics by any means but it was better than nothing. There was nothing for pain.

This young man had his arm amputated four days earlier, was walking around somewhere now and didn't have any pain medication. It was then that I noticed the tape. He had a piece of tape on his head that said OR-1. I asked him where he was staying and he told me that he was at his house. But the tape was still on. I then realized that he had been walking around the city with this piece of tape on that told his triage status.

As a nurse, I found the "tape system" something difficult to bear. I understood the need for immediate recognition of people's needs in an emergency situation. I understood that we didn't have time to talk to everyone and needed to determine priorities for care quickly. But the situation itself seemed so dehumanizing. People lying on the floor, on pieces of cardboard, outside under sheets supported by sticks, on ragged mattresses. Having a piece of tape on your forehead, now five days after being treated just seemed too much.

I attempted to try to take the tape off of him. But at this point it was stuck on so tightly I couldn't get it off without causing him yet more pain. So I just left it, told him he could take it off when he got home and went to find some pain medication.

My thinking was that I could find some pain medication for this young man, give it to him, have him wait a bit, allowing the pain medication to take effect while I could see another patient or two and then proceed on to his dressing change.

This was my first contact with the pharmacy that was set up at HCH. Fortunately the room was immediately adjacent to my courtyard zone. Two Haitian women were sitting in this small room that was filled to the brim with boxes. They had many small zip lock bags on the counter and were filling them with 30 Tylenol (paracetamol as it is known in many European and foreign countries). I asked them what they had for pain medication. The one appeared to be a nurse or some formal employee of the hospital as was noted by a form of a nametag. The other one was dressed in street clothes and was talking on a cell phone. A volunteer was working in the pharmacy-yet another example of the dysfunctional government which provided no oversight to health care provision in Haiti-disaster or not.

Nothing appeared organized. The boxes contained many types of supplies but were in no semblance of order. Some were half opened and looked like they had been rifled through to find something. Others were just stacked up, the contents of them unknown at this time. If we didn't know what was in them, how useful could their contents be to us? Oh well...

On the one counter space which served as the work area, were numerous bottles of medication. Most of them looked like over the counter type medication. Some were large bottles of prescription drugs, mostly common antibiotics.

She told me in broken English that she had this-and thrust a small zip lock bag into my hands. It contained about 20 Tylenol pills. I asked her did she have any morphine or anything stronger. She couldn't understand what I said. So I grabbed a translator who was working in the triage area directly next to the pharmacy and asked him to ask her if she had morphine or anything stronger than Tylenol. She looked carefully around, trying really hard to be helpful-unlike the woman on the cell phone-and pulled out a large bottle of Advil.

She looked at me expectantly and said, "We have this."

This situation came to represent the absurdity of what we were dealing with. A natural disaster of catastrophic proportions and I was handed Ibuprofen to deal with pain from the injuries. I was to come to find out later that this kind of situation was commonplace. A friend would write to me months later about her own similar experience:

"We were forced to perform procedures under local anesthesia that I am still haunted by".

From my perspective Ibuprofen was no better than Tylenol. This man was going to have serious pain when I tried to take this dressing off and those kinds of drugs wouldn't put a dent in it. Needing to think quickly, and seeing what the resources we had-which were sparse and adequate- and knowing that time was of the essence-I decided to take the Tylenol and returned back to the patient.

I told him I didn't have any stronger pain medication and asked him if I could give him some of this and wait a few minutes. He agreed to take the Tylenol but said he thought he could endure the dressing change if I wanted to go ahead with it. I was reluctant but seeing the many patients still to be evaluated, I decided to acquiesce to his wishes. In the back of my mind, I knew if I decided to delay him, other priorities might come up and he wouldn't get any care. So I made one of the first hard decisions that day and went forward with a less than ideal plan. I knew at least he would get the care he needed, although he would suffer needlessly in the process.

These are the kinds of decisions that one must make nearly every minute in disaster work. The balancing of seeing as many people as you can while trying to prioritize needs and knowing that the care may not be what you might desire as an ideal, but knowing that they will get safe care, is a process that I would go through a thousand times that day. Over time, it takes a toll.
I dispensed 3 Tylenol-an extra one to help with the pain I knew he would feel after the dressing change was over. I had to take the dressing off. There was a lot of drainage on it and that concerned me. I needed to see what was underneath it.

I began the pain process of taking the tape off and unwinding the gauze dressing. Surgeons usually put fresh post-op dressing on pretty securely. Most of the time they don't want the wound disturbed for at least two days to allow the healing to begin and to prevent any infection causing bacteria from the outside world to get to the wound.

The amputation was high above the elbow, leaving only about 10 inches of his arm from the shoulder. He needed to lift the stump to allow me to remove the dressing. As I unwrapped the dressing, I saw his face grimace several times, making it harder for me to continue. But I knew it was necessary.

Once the dressing was unwrapped, I realized I didn't have a place to put the old dressing. I was becoming frustrated with the lack of resources available to me. I quickly spotted an empty trash bag across the courtyard. I wrapped the old dressing into a tight ball, and carried it carefully across the courtyard to the bag. I grabbed the bag, put the dressing in it, and took it back to my zone.

The stump still had a couple of gauze pads covering the actual incision area. So I removed them. What I saw nearly made me gasp. To understand that reaction, you will need to know that I am a seasoned professional, having over thirty years of experience in health care and nearly 10 years of providing medical care in Haiti. I have seen many horrible looking wounds over my long career. Infections were something I was accustomed to seeing. I have also been privy to lots of third world medicine.

What I saw was the start of my clear understanding of the depth of this tragedy. This was to begin my patient relief work involving patient care in the aftermath of the Haitian earthquake. The young man's stump was sutured together only with three very large sutures or stitches. To be frank, it looked like something that a child might have done in a pre-school project where they had a large needle with some yarn. The edges of the skin weren't even brought together. This process is called, in medical terms, approximated. Approximating the edges (bringing them together through the use of sutures) allows the skin to begin to grow together just by the fact that each edge is touching the other.

Additionally, the wound was clearly infected. There was a large amount of yellow drainage coming from the wound. I could clearly see the fascia. Fascia is a bodily substance which interpenetrates and surrounds muscles, bones, organs, nerves, blood vessels and other structures. It is responsible for maintaining structural integrity, providing support and protection and acts as a shock absorber for the body. It is not something that one should see through a wound incision. Below the fascia, I saw clearly the muscle of this young man's upper arm exposed through the wound.

I wasn't sure who did this surgery, but the technique was less than ideal. Clearly the wound was infected now and needed additional surgery to revise the stump to get the wound in a position where it actually would heal.

91

As horrible as this situation was, I knew that this problem ranked lower on the priority scale than some others that were in the other zones and likely others that we would see that day where immediate care was needed to save someone's life or those who were already waiting to be seen. For medical professionals who had less experience in acknowledging their limitations or determining what priorities were third world type medicine, my experience had been that much time is wasted trying to do things that they cannot do, wish they could do, or could do if they were in their own clinics at home.

I knew this young man needed further surgery but he would not be seen as a priority today. I reviewed this case with the triage physician and we agreed that my plan was the best. I would irrigate and clean the wound, start him on a more appropriate form of antibiotics, and have him return in two days to be seen again. He currently did not have a fever so I didn't have any reason to think the infection was spreading. With the use of more appropriate antibiotics, hopefully this would be prevented. We would not want to take an infected wound to the operating room. If the infection could be cleared up some, it would make any further surgery more likely to be successful in starting the healing process and having a good long term result.

I was also beginning to worry about the time I had spent on this one patient when, now as I looked at the triage area, there were now several hundred patients there-all of whom had come in the last 40 minutes it had taken me to just evaluate what needed to be done on this one patient.

With that plan in mind, I went, yet again, to the supply room. This was my fifth trip in just 30 minutes. I needed something to irrigate this wound. I found an IV bag and grabbed it. Since there were no beds in the triage area and the only place to lay down was on the floor, I asked the woman who was with this young man to help me by holding the absorbent pad underneath his remaining arm while I poured the sterile liquid over it, washing away any, and providing a clean environment for the tissue to begin to heal.

This also caused grimacing but through my translator, I just asked him to hold on and it would be over soon. It wasn't the best way to do this procedure but the result was what I wanted-a clean wound and something I felt comfortable putting a new dressing on.

I put a large amount of triple antibiotic cream on the wound, redressed it with a sterile dressing and taped it up. This process of applying the new dressing went rather quickly and as I might have expected with no unexpected circumstances. I breathed a sigh of relief. At least something went the way I had planned.
I found a syringe, an alcohol pad and gave him his tetanus shot. My last part of the plan was to change the antibiotics. I located the Keflex that I needed easily in the pharmacy and dispensed two full weeks of pills. I instructed him to take them three times a day.

As I handed him the envelope with the drugs in it, the young man, who had endured this process so stoically and with such dignity, turned to me and asked "How much is this going to cost?"

My heart was broken at this statement. How terribly sad that after this whole difficult process, the first thing on his mind was how he would pay for it. This was understandable from my perspective.

I explained to him that all of the care given at this hospital was going to be free. He didn't have to worry about paying for anything now or for any of his foreseeable future visits. All of the relief workers were there to help and we weren't charging for our services. He seemed so relieved.

Once I collected myself from this interaction, I jotted my findings and what I did for him today down on his "chart"-two pieces of paper detailing what had happened to him previously-and gave it back to him with instructions to bring this back when he returned in two days to have someone look at it again. My experience with previous clinics in Haiti is that the Haitians are very reliable with maintaining these kinds of records outside the hospital/clinic setting. They will move heaven and earth to keep those kinds of things safe and rarely show up back at the clinic without them.

I asked him if he had any questions- all this through my translator- he said "no" and then went on his way.

This whole process had taken 55 minutes. I knew I could not keep this slow pace up the rest of the day without potentially sacrificing the care that so many other patients needed. I needed a newer and better plan. And that had to come soon.

Patient in the Tent Hospital area awaiting surgery on her fractured leg

Chapter 7
Reunion with Beloved Friends

My next patient was a young woman who came in being carried by her husband. She was 36 years old. Her brought her in and laid her on the floor since it was impossible for her to put any weight on her leg. I took her papers and saw that her problem was inability to bear weight on her leg after being hit by a falling wall. She had not sought medical care until today-now 8 days after the earthquake-the reason was unclear. We had heard that many patients were trying to get care for their injuries but had not been able to at some hospitals and were traveling to a different one each day hoping to get seen.

She didn't have any broken area on her skin and no obvious wounds. I felt her left thigh which was obviously swollen. She clearly had pain when I touched it. I suspected that her femur-the thigh bone-was broken. How serious, it was hard to tell.

Since she had no other injuries, I thought we should first get an e-ray and see what that showed. The process of getting an x-ray was a complex one. I had to fill out a small piece of paper, give it to one of the many volunteer transporters who were helping out and they had to find a way to transport the patient to the x-ray machine. Once the x-ray was done, the patient would be returned to the zone, the x-ray evaluated and further treatment determined.

The young men who served as transporters were just some of the many volunteers from the community who had come to assist in the disaster efforts. They had just come to the hospital asking if they would be used in some helpful manner. Yvonne assigned the able bodied men to assist with moving patients when needed

The glitch in this system was the transport. On our first day at HCH, the transport system was far from refined. The biggest problem was that there was nothing to transport the patient on. There were only a couple of wheelchairs available and no rolling gurneys or stretchers. There were a couple of military type canvas stretchers but those were almost always in use.

Since transport to the x-ray was going to take some time, I didn't feel that I could just wait for that to happen. I asked one of the transporters to assist my patient and move her to a makeshift holding area on the grass in the middle of the courtyard near my zone. She obviously was in severe pain. I found an IV bag and tubing as well as the IV catheter needed to insert the IV. I started an IV on her to help replace some fluids and allow access in the event I could locate some pain medication to give her through the IV.

She had a green blanket with her. We instructed her husband to place that on the ground in an area next to the small tropical tree where she could be shaded. Since the courtyard was open air, the sun was beating down through the top of the area. Shade was a luxury. Prior to moving her to the "holding area" I hadn't thought about what to do with the bag of IV fluids. But once I went to check on her a few minutes later, I saw one of the images that will define this whole Haitian experience for me.

After moving the patient to the designated area, the transporter had hung the IV bag on a broken branch of the tree. Here, in the middle of one of the largest natural disasters in human history, was a sign that people were working to help others in whatever fashion available-an IV bag hanging from a tree branch. It was resourceful, served the purpose exactly and used what was available to meet the goal. I quickly grabbed my camera which I kept in my pocket near me for just these kinds of purposes, and snapped a picture of it. It will stay in my mind forever and will be shown to each person or group that I speak to about this experience.

It was clear that I was going to need pain medication for patients so I felt I needed to take some time and search out where I could find some. I checked again at the pharmacy. They just gave me the Advil and Tylenol. So I decided to make my way up to the larger supply depot and see if maybe there was some there. Yvonne had pointed to an area on the upper floor of the building which surrounded the open courtyard in her tour but hadn't given us specific directions to it.

I found a flight of stairs adjacent to the lobby and made my way up. Right at the top on the left was an open area which had been walled off at waist high level with several rows of boxes to make a counter of sorts. Behind this counter was the supply area.

There were 3 or 4 people in there. The room was full of supplies. I was astonished to see all of the supplies that were in this area. What was disheartening was that there was no semblance of order to it at all. I saw many boxes partially opened with some materials which had been taken from them. There were numerous other boxes not opened so we had no way to determine what was in them. Small, shoe box size boxes of gloves were strewn everywhere with gloves hanging out of them. It was clear that many people had needed gloves as a mainstay of their care provision.

I had no idea of how to procure supplies or the medication that I needed. One of the volunteers came over when he saw me standing at the cardboard counter looking puzzled.

"Can I get something for you?" he said with a friendly smile.

This man was a volunteer from one of the rescue teams, a white man. His tape name tag said his name was Tom. There were no credentials after it so I assumed he wasn't a medical professional.

OK. So this is how this works, I thought. Pretty simple. I just tell them what I need. I told him I needed some morphine. Is this where I come to get it?

He seemed so eager to help. He located a box and his expression seemed to indicate that was what I needed and I was thrilled. Was it really that easy? He proceeded to pick up the whole box- a standard shipping box about 24 x 24- and brought it to me. Inside the box were many smaller boxes about the size of a bar of soap.

He began to push the large box towards me and said, "Is this what you want?"

Those of you who are reading this who are in the medical field will understand my response. This man was ready to give me an entire case of morphine vials!

I asked him to set it on the box counter and opened up one of the smaller boxes inside. Truly, it was morphine. Each of the smaller boxes contained 20 ampoules of morphine in a concentration of 1 mg per milliliter-about one teaspoon.

This man was ready to give me several hundred ampoules of morphine—just like that! I told him kindly that I didn't need the whole thing but would take one of the smaller boxes-better get it while I could. This was just another example of the chaotic nature of things in this country where there existed no governmental infrastructure to protect people on any level. How could a lay person be in possession of a box of hundreds of ampoules of a narcotic with no oversight, signatures required, or monitoring of any kind? One needs no imagination at all to see how the potential problems with this situation could lead to illegal activity and just how easily that could have occurred.

Oh well…at least I got what I needed. I couldn't think about the bigger issues at that point.

My patient was in pain and needed this medication. I took the 20 ampoules and stuck them in my pocket-something I was mildly uncomfortable with- but it was what was needed at this particular time. I got the necessary medication and finally gave her the morphine she needed to get some relief now 8 days after her injury. It was amazing to me that this was the first medical care she had received.

I was beginning to see how every little thing was now going to be something that required a major energy outlay. Nothing was to come easily and we were really going to have to work for every little bit of care we provided—and work hard.

When I returned from the little oasis where the IV was hanging from the tree branch, I noticed that one of the Hungarian doctors on our team was seeing patients in Zone 4 now. There wasn't really room for two people in that small area so I decided to see if I could be useful in one of the post op rooms while I waited for the woman under the tree to get her x-ray.

While walking down the hallway, I heard someone call my name in Kreyol-"Avril" (pronounced Ah-vreel).

Was I hearing things? I turned around to see one of my dear friends from Haiti-Eddy Petit Homme!

Eddy had worked with us for many years. He was one of my favorite translators. He was 32 years old and lived in Cite Soleil, a slum located right in the middle of Port au Prince.

Cite Soleil is generally regarded as one of the poorest and most dangerous areas of the Western Hemisphere's poorest country. It is one of the biggest slums in the Northern Hemisphere. Over 200,000 people live in 4 square miles. There is little police presence, no sewers, no stores, and little to no electricity. The houses are all shanties made out of corrugated tin and tree branches that support a rickety roof.

The neighborhood, originally designed by Madame Duvalier, to house manual laborers for a local Export Processing Zone (EPZ), quickly became home to squatters from around the countryside who were looking for work in the newly constructed factories. After a 1991 coup d'état deposed President Jean-Bertrand Aristide for the first time, a boycott of Haitian products closed the EPZ. Cité Soleil was soon thrust into extreme poverty and persistent unemployment, with high rates of illiteracy.

In 1999, Cité Soleil was set on fire by a gang and at least 50 shacks were burned. During mid-1990s, the city's population was terrorized by armed gangs, based in Cite Soleil, which drove the local police out; this situation prevented official aid workers from intervening to provide help. In subsequent years, the violence escalated as the Cite Soleil gangs began warring with each other, in addition to preying on ordinary people. Many inhabitants left temporarily to escape the turmoil.

In the early part of the twenty first century, Cite Soleil remained a central haven for the gangs, especially during the 2004 revolution and coup d'état. Following the second forced departure of Aristide, the president of Haiti, in 2004 UN peacekeepers stormed Cité Soleil in an attempt to gain control of the area and end the anarchy that had developed.

In the next two years, gangs would control and terrorize this area. I knew several people in the church we worked in who were murdered as a result of gang violence in Cite Soleil. MINUSTAH-the UN United Nations Stabilization Mission peacekeeping force which had been occupying Haiti since 2004-maintained an armed checkpoint at the entrance to Cité Soleil and the road was often blocked with armed vehicles. Until 2008, armed gangs roamed the streets. Murder, rape, kidnapping, looting, and shootings were common as every few blocks were controlled by one of more than 30 armed factions. The area has been called a "microcosm of all the ills in Haitian society-- endemic unemployment, illiteracy, non-existent public services, unsanitary conditions, rampant crime, and armed violence.

Since the MINUSTAH has been deployed in 2004, through strong and forceful efforts, most of the gangs have departed from Cite Soleil so the day to day violence has decreased. However, it remains the largest and poorest slum on this half of the earth.

We had been working in Cite Soleil for 8 years with several Christian pastors who had thriving church works there. We had encountered violence on a couple of occasions and always were extremely cautious going there. However, when Shelia and I had been there only three months before the earthquake, we felt that the situation in Haiti, as a whole, was the best we had seen in years. We felt safe walking unescorted in the streets around out guest house. The governmental services such as electricity and trash pickup were a little better and the police presence, along with the UN, was clear and evident. Crime was significantly down in Cite Soleil and the gangs no longer ruled there. A new paved street was now located through the middle of the slum area.

We had many friends in Cite Soleil. In fact most of our friends in the Port au Prince area lived in Cite Soleil. Eddy was no different. When I saw his face, and realized that he was really alive and well, my heart skipped a few beats.

"Eddy", I cried out as I ran to him and hugged him tightly.
I was especially concerned to see Eddy because he was Bosie's best friend. I knew he would be grieving deeply. So it was a bittersweet moment.

I asked him how he was doing. He told me that it had been really hard for him and his family. No one had been killed but they could not live in their home and were staying on the street---- sleeping there. He said they were all very sad. He told me that when I saw the rest of the city it would make me cry like he did. We didn't have a lot of time to catch up. I had patients to see. So I asked him if he wanted to work with me for the day.

"Of course", was his response.

I had been using the volunteer translators who were slowing me down, so having my own translator would be a real treat.

I quickly told him what the situation was and what we were doing in the hospital. He agreed to stay with me for the day. I had brought money with me, hoping I would be able to provide some of our fiends with a job for the week while being able to spend some time with them as well.

Nandor, the Hungarian doctor, now working in Zone 4 had several patients there. After I found the morphine, I decided to see if I could help out in the post op wards. I grabbed Eddy and we headed off to the first room serving post op patients. There was no medical care provider at all in the room.

OK. I would just start at the beginning and work my way around the room. The first lady was lying on the floor on a piece of cardboard. Her husband was with her, also sitting on the floor. They both looked expectantly at me as I asked if she had been seen by a doctor today. She shook her head no.

I quickly looked at her paper. She had a large dressing on her right hand. The notes indicated that she had three fingers amputated following "the event"-as the earthquake was now repeatedly being translated by our interpreters. Other than that she looked fairly well. I asked her if there were any other problems to which she said no.

Her dressing was noted to be changed today. It seemed to me that she didn't have any other reason to stay so I asked if she wanted to go home after I changed the dressing. To my surprise both she and her husband said yes.

Yet again I went on the hunt for the materials to change the dressing. Her dressing was small enough so that I could change it without serious pain. After locating all of the things I needed, I found a chair and sat down on the floor to be more at her level. I placed an absorbent underpad on my lap and asked her to put her hand up there. There was nothing else to use as a work surface except my lap.

When I removed the dressing, her hand showed that there was now only the ring finger and pinkie left. I didn't get a chance to ask her exactly what happened to leave her without her fingers. The incision line looked clean enough, although again the surgical technique left much to be desired. Her thumb was still present which was fortunate for her since the thumb provides over half of the functional ability of a hand. There was no sign of infection. As I changed the dressing, I did a figure eight wrap, trying to place the new dressing on so she would have some use of the thumb.

It seemed like I might actually be able to discharge someone. I saw that she had been on doxycycline also-the same antibiotic that the first patient had been on. It seems like the supply of cephalosporins-the standard post operative antibiotics- had been used up requiring this other kind of antibiotic to be used. I gave her the Keflex with instructions on how to take it and told her that I thought if she wanted to, she could go home. Both she and her husband were affirmative in their desire to do so. I signed off on her paperwork, gave it to her and told her to keep it with her when she returned here in 5 days for someone to check her again. I couldn't believe it. The first patient I saw, I was actually able to discharge.

Eddy and I continued around the room. There were several other patients with amputations-fingers, hands, lower legs. All needed dressing changes and checks on the medication they were taking. Several had deep wounds which needed to be checked and redressed. On was a father who had lost his foot and his son who had lost his lower leg; both were sharing a bed because there was no other place for them.

In the far corner was a little girl; one of the few children in this hospital. She had a broken leg. She had on an external fixator . I noticed her particularly because she was lying on a thin mattress on the floor with her father beside her. Another thing which caught my attention was she had her leg with the fixator on it propped up on her father's knee but she was having a very animated conversation on a cell phone. To me, seeing that little girl carrying on a cell phone conversation represented some semblance of normalcy in this world of chaos.

It took Eddy and me about two hours to see the 15 or so patients in that room. I had to go look for everything I needed for each patient. There didn't seem to be any central place where supplies could be kept and that was frustrating to me. More than once Eddy served as an assistant for whatever I needed with the patient-supporting a limb while I changed the dressing, serving as an extra set of hands to get the dressing material on or off correctly. He was a godsend to me. There was still no nurse or other health care provider in that room. That concerned me. But there were others that needed care and these people seemed to be OK for the moment. So we proceeded on to the areas further back in the hospital.

April changes a dressing while sitting on the floor of the hospital

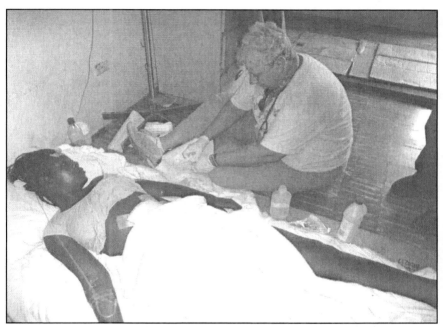

Building collapse in Petionville

Chapter 8
Post Op

The back of the hospital where the rest of the post operative patients were was more than what one might expect to see in a typical Haitian hospital. There were three small rooms which would normally hold 3-4 patients each. A nurse's station was located in a central area in the larger area outside the three patient rooms.

Eddy and I proceeded back to this area. I saw a lot of activity but it didn't seem like there were any health care providers around. Instead of the normal 3-4 patients each room was intended to hold, there were more like 8-10. As with the previous room, patients were lying on the floor when beds were not available. None of the patients had seen a doctor that day so we just started making our rounds with the patient closest to the door.

This was a 12 year old boy-one of the three pediatric patients at HCH. He was lying in a bed with his mother and another family member nearby. I noticed him right away because he was crying hard. His right leg showed a below the knee amputation about half way down his lower leg. A large dressing was on his stump.

I worked with Eddy to find out what was wrong and why he was crying. I noticed this boy quickly because I had been surprised at the lack of emotional response by the Haitians to the situation the earthquake had caused in the 5 hours I had been there. I believed that they were still in shock and trying to grasp the enormity of the situation which led to a lack of overt emotional response. So this boy's tears were something that I hadn't seen before during that day.

106

He was clearly in pain. His mother said that his leg hurt very badly. I looked at it and didn't see anything that caused me any specific concern; no drainage on the dressing; the circulation looked good. His surgery had been the day before so I would have expected this to be normal post operative pain. Looking at his papers, I saw that he had not had any pain medication today—it was now 1:00 PM.

Fortunately I still had the remainder of the small box of morphine vials in my pocket I had obtained earlier in the day. I was concerned giving him IV morphine. He was young but I could adjust the dose to account for that. Most Haitians have never had any kind of medication on a regular basis simply because they cannot afford it. When giving medical care in Haiti I am always concerned about allergies to medications. These wouldn't be documented anywhere and the Haitian's may not have known that they had an allergic response to a medication if a health care provider hadn't told them.

Of more concern was the fact that very few Haitians had ever had any kind of strong pain medication like morphine. This situation in medical terms is called "opioid naïve". Simply stated, it means that the person has never had opioids-morphine like narcotics. As a result they may respond with side effects to even small doses.

This little boy clearly needed strong pain medication but I needed to be careful because I was sure he was opioid naïve. I figured out what dose I needed to give him and decided to give him half of that dose to see how he responded to it. I could always give more but I couldn't control side effects once they started until the drug wore off.

I told his mom that we were going to give him some strong pain medication to help his pain. She understood and expressed her gratitude.

I checked on the other patients in the room. Most had surgery the day before, needed dressing changes and antibiotics. By this time it was nearly 2 PM. I was very hot and tired. So I took Eddy and we went to the area designated for the relief workers to get some water and food.

Somehow, someway, food appeared in the upstairs area each day. It was simple food—bread, lunch meat or cheese and bottled water. There was all the bottled water that we needed. We were free to take anything there we needed. Additionally in a room which was designated for the relief workers, there was a small microwave and many cases of MRE's- meals ready to eat- the kind of vacuum packed food that soldiers often eat.

This room was where those staying on the premises were keeping their belongings. It was filled with suitcases, duffle bags, air mattresses, pillows and other personal items. Each time we went in this room, several people could be seen on their computers sending or checking their emails. The hospital did have Internet service via a satellite.

We took a few minutes among other workers there to grab an MRE and a bottle of water. There were several other relief workers in the room and a reporter or two. Now that I had stopped, I realized how tired I was. I had been on my feet all day without stopping since we arrived nearly 7 hours before. I took a couple minutes to text the following message back home:

> *"This morning- Port au Prince better than I thought.*
> *Hospital UNBELIEVABLE. The hospital is full plus a*
> *tent city hospital for 100 outside. More later.*
> *Under His crushing mercy,*
> *April*

There were relief teams at HCH from several countries-the United States, Korea and Sweden. All totaled, there were about 50 relief workers and many volunteers from the community working at HCH when we arrived the first day. The Swedish team was made up of mostly surgeons. They kept the OR's running about 18 hours a day. The Korean team was comprised of some doctors, nurses and a number of paramedics working in the other zones of the triage. I would notice these other relief teams in passing but much of the work I was doing was on my own. It seemed like there needed to be some organization of the relief workers to accomplish more in the time we had.

I also realized I had not seen any of my team members at all for much of the day. I assumed they were located in other areas of the hospital doing what they were assigned to do. As I had the first few minutes to think about how the day had gone so far, I began to realize how much time I had spent looking for things I needed. Supplies were located in various places and nothing was centralized. It was clear that I would need a lot more of the same kinds of supplies I had used for the many dressing changes I had done that day. These included, gauze bandages, rolled gauze called Kerlix, tape, hydrogen peroxide, alcohol swabs, sterile water and gloves. Any dressing I changed, I would need these supplies.

I decided that it was worth the time investment to try to organize supplies in order to utilize my time more efficiently. When we finished our short break, Eddy and I went on the lookout for a cart or something that I could use to store supplies for dressing changes. I found a small old rolling cart with a drawer in the front of it back in the corner of a supply room which wasn't being used. This seemed perfect for what I was thinking of doing.

I wheeled the cart down to the one supply room where some of the dressing supplies were located and put as many of those things on the cart as I thought it could hold. Then I went to another area where some tape, irrigation fluid, hydrogen peroxide and Kerlix were located. I loaded the cart up with those things. Finally I went up to the larger supply area upstairs and got the things that I was missing. This all had taken about 30 minutes but I knew in the long run would save me countless minutes and maybe hours of time allowing me to see more patients.

I wheeled the cart back down to the back post op area of the hospital and began to see the rest of the patients in the other two rooms. At this time of day, more people had come hoping to be seen by the health care providers. I saw a couple of Haitian nurses sitting behind the nurse's station. Now when I needed medications, they had a supply there and could get them for me quickly. There also seemed to be more relief workers coming in as the day progressed.

One patient I saw was a middle aged Haitian woman who was sitting in a hallway. She had a small cot type bed with a thin mattress on it. Her bed was pushed up against a short metal storage cabinet so she could sit on the bed and lean her back against the cabinet. The reason this was important was because both of her arms were broken. She had casts from her wrist to her shoulders on both arms. Of course she couldn't move either of her arms at all and she looked like the Michelin Tire man with her arms extended out slightly from her body. She looked completely miserable.

When I got to her, I asked her daughter for her papers. I asked her how she was feeling. She indicated she was in a lot of pain. She had just had her casts placed on the day before so it was to be expected she would be in some pain. I remembered the remaining vials of morphine I still had tucked in my pocket from the morning. I looked at her papers and saw that she had morphine the day before but nothing today. I asked her if she was eating and drinking OK to which she responded yes, as did her daughter. She had some food with her in the little metal tins that Haitian's often carry around with them. It is typical for Haitians to carry small portions of food around with them in these.

She didn't have an IV. It would have been better to give her something orally. I checked with the nurses at the desk and with the pharmacy but the only oral pain medication they still had were the non prescription ones I had been told of that morning. Eddy helped me explain to her that I could give her some strong pain medication but I would need to give it to her as a shot because she didn't have an IV. The only place to give it to her would be in her thighs because her arms were not accessible.

I also explained to her that it might make her sleepy to which she responded that would be OK. I don't like giving morphine in an injection. It doesn't work as well and giving it by IV is preferable. But this was the situation that had presented itself to me and I had to work with it—as I had with many other situations during the day. She wasn't a thin woman so there was plenty of muscle on her thighs in which to give it. And she did look miserable with both of those casts, her arms sticking out needing someone to do everything for her. She couldn't even lie down comfortably which was why they had found this cabinet to locate her bed in front of. I gave her the shot, hoping it would work, and told her daughter I would be back later to check on her.

I noticed the time. It was now 3:30. We were supposed to meet at the front of the hospital at 4:30 to depart for the day. I had about an hour to finish up seeing the patients in the back area. I hoped I would have time to complete that before time for us to leave. I had probably seen 40 patients in all that day. As we passed the room where the little boy with the amputated foot was, the one I had given pain medication to earlier, I heard him. He was still crying. I stuck my head in and saw another nurse in there whom I had not seen before. She was a Haitian American nurse who had just arrived later that day and was helping out as well. I asked her what was wrong with him and she told me he was still in a lot of pain. I told her I had given him some morphine earlier. She said she realized that had and she had just given him some more.

I wondered if he was having phantom limb pain. Phantom limb pain is the sensation that an amputated or missing limb is still attached to the body and is experiencing pain. Approximately 5 to 10% of individuals with an amputation experience phantom sensations in their amputated limb, and the majority of the sensations are painful. This pain is real.

I discussed this with her but was really getting concerned about the degree of pain this little boy was having. She agreed and said she was going to find the surgeon who did his surgery and talk to him about it. That seemed like a good plan so I continued to try to finish up seeing the rest of the patients.

Heat and fatigue were catching up with me now. I began to feel extremely tired. We ran upstairs again to get some water. As the day progressed, the heat became worse. In the back part of the hospital there was little ventilation-unlike the open air courtyard where I started out. My back was also hurting. I knew it was more of a stress kind of pain in my upper shoulders than something else. It had been a stressful and trying day.

I looked at my watch and saw it was 4:25. I had no idea where my other team mates were but thought I probably should wind up what I was doing and try to make it to the meeting point on time. I finished up the documentation on the last patient-a woman who had just had surgery today for a broken arm and had external fixators on her lower arm. She seemed to be OK. Her pain was controlled but she needed a new IV bag. The one she had was almost out. I thought I could quickly just hang a new one before I left. I got the new one and hung it.

But it wouldn't drip. In the United States we use machines to control the IV flow rates on nearly all IV's. When I was a young nurse, we didn't have those so I learned how to calculate how fast an IV was dripping by counting the drops in the chamber per minute. You could adjust the rate by knowing how many drops per minute. I opened the clamp up all the way allowing it to flow as wide open as it could but still nothing.

Great-the last thing I was doing that day- a simple thing like changing an IV bag-and it was becoming complicated. I needed to go out to find a syringe, and something to flush the line with. That wasn't easy. The simplest things in the United States, things I wouldn't even really have to think about and that were second nature, here in the Haiti were time consuming and frustrating. It took a few minutes again to find what I needed. I had to work with the woman's IV line several minutes to get it going. But I was finally able to leave it running at about the rate she needed. My patience was beginning to run thin now.

It was now 4:50 PM. I was late. Before I left, I remembered the box of morphine in my pocket. I decided to put it in a safe place where I could find it the next day, knowing I would need it and hoping I wouldn't have to use precious time looking for more. I tucked it in the back of a drawer behind a bunch of other supplies at the nurse's desk. Given the chaotic circumstances that prevailed, I was fairly certain no one would find it and I would know exactly where it was the next day. I ran by the woman with the two broken arms on my way toward the front entrance where we were to meet. She was sleeping soundly. I asked her daughter if she seemed OK and she nodded affirmatively. So I thought she would be OK, for a while anyway.

With that final check, Eddy and I made our way up to the front of the hospital. The triage area was less crowded with new patients but many more patients were now lying around the edges filling up nearly every available floor space. The woman I had seen earlier in the day with the broken femur was still lying under the tree with her IV hanging from a branch. I checked later with our team doctor who was overseeing her now. He said she would have surgery later in the evening. I said good bye to Eddy and asked him if he would come back tomorrow to work with me.

He said, "Of course" and left to go home.

I was so grateful for him.

Several of my team mates were waiting at the door. A couple more came within the next few minutes. Because the mission compound had a schedule for the meals they served us and all the other relief workers staying there, it was important that we maintain the schedule they had. Their staff couldn't wait around for us to come in late.

I also knew the real dangers of being on the road after dark in Haiti. People and animals were often all over the roads, there were no street lights anywhere and it was more dangerous at night in general. I thought it was important to get back before dark regardless of the schedule.

Several of my team mates expressed frustration at having to leave with things still left to do. I realized that there would always be "things left to do" no matter when we left—for months to come—so waiting until you thought you were "done" seemed pointless to me. There were other things for us to consider and we needed to get back to the compound.

We all boarded the van which was waiting for us. We were a little late leaving but likely would be back to the mission compound in time for the dinner which was served from 6-7 PM.

I didn't say much on the 45 minute ride back to the Global Outreach Mission compound. I was so tired. But also, it was the first time I had had to really think about what I had seen that day. The sheet shanty hospital rooms outside-the first impression of what we were getting in to-so many sick people, people injured, in need of care, so many amputations, a lack of supplies and equipment, the heat, the crowded and dehumanizing conditions, people lying on the floors, the tape on the young man's forehead. It was exhausting me to think about it.

As we pulled up into the compound, we unloaded right at the mess hall and went directly in to get our supper. The meals here were good-simple but filling. That night we had spaghetti, bread and salad. The most wonderful thing at this compound was ice. They had ice and plenty of it. The water we drank was actually cold—something which I have found to be a luxury in Haiti. Cold water does so much more to refresh than other bottled water.

Most of my team mates felt like talking a lot that evening. That was good because I just really didn't have much to say. My mind was still trying to process all I had seen. I had a context into which to put this. I knew what Port au Prince looked like before. I knew what these hospitals were like and what they were capable of. I knew some of these people. I knew people who had died and others who were in other places in the city who were seriously injured.

Our team leader wanted to have a meeting at 8:00 PM to talk about the schedule for the next day. I really didn't want to go. So I decided I would shower and be already to go to bed when that was over. I was really completely exhausted—some of it physical but a great deal of it was mental exhaustion.

In the meeting we had a vigorous discussion about the pros and cons of doing 24 hour shifts at the hospital-the idea that the previous team had brought up to us the evening before. We did see that there were far fewer relief workers available during the night time. We knew there was a need but I didn't see that staying for 24 hours was the way to meet it. I indicated I would be glad to do overnight shifts and come in at the end of the afternoon to do so, but staying 24 hours and then returning to the compound for the next day to sleep didn't seem to make sense to me.

As a mission team leader I have found that people who have not encountered these kinds of situations often want to put every ounce of effort they have into it without consideration for the implications and results. I was already exhausted. I wasn't sure how effective or, more importantly, how safe I would be for another 12 hours. I offered again to do overnights and return but I made it clear that is seemed short sighted to wear one's self out especially early in the week when so much else had to be done.

However, a number of the people on my team were what one typically considers Type A personalities, pushing forward under any circumstances. We finally decided that those who did want to do 24 hours would do so (mostly all of the doctors and paramedics) and the van would bring the rest of us-the other two nurses and myself back. I talked to the missionary nurse at the compound about this later. She completely agreed with the logic I had stated and thought it showed great wisdom.

As a team leader when I lead mission teams, I consider it my responsibility to reign in these kinds of feelings and try to help people understand what their limitations are. We won't save the world this week; we won't even save Haiti; we might help some people but there will be plenty left to do when we leave whether we burn ourselves out for Jesus or not. I was mostly concerned about the quality of the care that one might be giving under these circumstances when you were tired. But in a state of severe fatigue, mistakes can happen even under the best of circumstance. I wanted to do all I could to prevent that.

After the meeting, I went to the dorm, got under the mosquito net on my bed and pulled out my smart phone. I typed in the following message-unable to do any more but wanting to keep the folks back home aware of what I was doing:

> *"I have been working at a small, local emergency department doing triage and post op care in a 60 bed hospital. It is now holding 100 people inside and about 150 patients are outside in a makeshift tent, like shanties on Hospital Drive.*
>
> *I have seen many, many amputations of many young people. That is really sad considering that at present, there are very few rehabilitation services or prosthetics available in Haiti. The damage in the city is more localized than I imagined, but very bad. I was, however, encouraged that life still goes on with some markets open and people on the streets despite the long lines for food.*
>
> *I am VERY TIRED. It has been a long and very busy day.*
>
> *Under His crushing mercy,*
> *April*

After texting those words from my bed, I began praying that the Lord would continue to give me courage and strength to be the hands that He so desperately needed in this situation to meet the enormous needs that lay ahead. And then I drifted off into a sleep born of exhaustion.

Injured father and son sharing a bed in Petionville Community Hospital

Chapter 9
Just a cup of water...

I woke early the next morning-Friday. We were to have devotions at 6 AM. I was leading them. We wanted to try to get out early by 7 AM to avoid the traffic and arrive at the hospital by 8:30. I used Isaiah 58 for my devotions discussing what God really wants from us-not pretend worship but real efforts at worshipping him through helping those who are in need. In return we will be called the "rebuilder of walls". It seemed to fit our situation.

Several from the team planned to stay the night at the hospital. As we boarded they carried with them a few extra things. My hope was that because I knew what I was getting into today, I would be better prepared and could function more efficiently. I had a feeling things would continue to progressively get busier each day meaning that I had a short time to progress up the learning curve.

It was Friday. I knew that typically n Haiti this is one of the two market days. I was interested to see if the markets were functioning as they might on other days. That would give me a gauge of how much effect on the daily routine this catastrophe had had.

As our van drove through the area where the market usually is in Petionville, I was happy to see the normal multitude of colors, smells, and other sensory delights that accompany market day in Haiti. I love going to the markets in Haiti. All of the produce and fruit is painstakingly arranged by each seller to entice buyers to purchase from them. There are so many colors and varieties of food and spices; it is like a piece of art. On this particular day, I noticed a woman carrying a very large bunch of carrots, crowned with the green tops still on them, on her head. It was a picture that was so Haitian. For me it represented an attempt to return to the normal.

As we pulled up to the hospital, nothing had changed much in the hours that had passed since we left. We had decided to change roles a bit. Since I could be useful providing nursing care as well as evaluating patients and treating them, I felt that I would be better used in the post op wards. The Hungarian physicians would take my place in the triage area.

Once, inside, I saw Eddy who was waiting there for me. It was so reassuring to see him. I felt better having my own translator not having to try to round one up when I needed one. Additionally, I was happy to be able to provide him with some income for the week.

The overnight nursing staff on the "post op" ward was one single Physicians Assistant who was caring about 100 patients inside for the evening before. I ran into him as he was getting ready to leave. He was from Miami, Florida. There were many relief workers all over the city from Miami. Miami has a large Haitian American population. This gave the Miami medical care professionals an additional connection to this disaster. Most of the Miami team was staying at the hospital in their meager facilities.

He described how he took care of all of those patients-- "doing things in bulk". For example, he filled a wheelchair with IV fluid bags and went around changing those that were ready to be changed. He did the same thing with pain medications. It seemed the most efficient, if not the most compassionate way to make sure everything that needed to be done, got done.

That morning Eddy and I started by rounding on the post op ward checking everybody from the night before. Since I knew many of the patients from the day before it seemed easier and took less time. Most were doing well but needed dressing changes, pin care-cleaning of the pins holding the external fixators on those patient who had them, dispensing pain medication, IV changing or other needs tended to. It became clear that more patients were going to be coming as the day progressed. It seemed imperative that if possible, I should try to evaluate any patients who might be able to be discharged to home to do so. More planned surgeries were scheduled that day. In some ways this wasn't much different a scenario from a similar a surgical unit's at home-just different surroundings and more of it.

That became more of a challenge than I might have imagined. Many people were scared to return to their homes. They expressed terror about returning to their damaged home and would prefer to stay on the hospital property even if they couldn't stay inside. The government had put out radio announcement instructing all of the citizens of Port au Prince to not go into any buildings because of the damage but also because of continuing aftershocks. Additionally some had no homes to go to.

The tent city outside was growing daily with people we couldn't keep inside and who have to be "discharged" from the inside rooms which were needed for those who had surgery and were immediate post op.

In the smaller room that I started with yesterday, there were now a team of Swedish nurses and one doctor. They had devised a system for caring for these patients so my services weren't needed there. I was happy to see that.

I noticed that some of the nurses had come up with some make shift shelves made out of large pieces of cardboard sandwiched between concrete blocks. On them, were numerous supplies that they would need-dressing materials, IV fluids, some over the counter medications, etc. It was clear that other people were feeling the same frustration I felt yesterday and trying to get organized a bit.

There still weren't many patients in the triage area yet-we had made really good time and got to the hospital before 8 AM- so I went to the supply area where I was working the day before and started pulling some things together for the day. A Swedish doctor, one who was helping to care for the patients in the room next door, came in to the room I was in.

It was used as a casting room, I think, before the disaster. It was small-maybe 10 x 10 ft. There were some old records in there as well as a large amount of materials used for placing casts on patient. The Swedish doctor thought that it might make a decent patient room and could help alleviate the overcrowding in their room next door. As we talked, I told her I thought that was a great idea.

I agreed to try to clean it up and add one additional room for patients. I donned gloves, found a mop and broom and sent bout to clean up this room. At this point, skill sets didn't seem to be as important as doing what needed to be done. Eddy and I took about 45 minutes and cleaned the room up so that it could accommodate more patients.

We let the Swedish doctor know it was ready. When she came in to see it all cleaned up and ready, her broad smile told us how she felt. It may have seemed like a menial thing to clean up trash, sweep floors and wipe own counters. In disaster work, as in third world medicine, one needs to do what is required and not necessarily what you are trained to do.

I have found this to be the case in my own work in Haiti before the earthquake. As a health care provider in a highly technical and sophisticated sub specialty-Pediatric Cardiology-one of the most difficult things for me to learn was to recognize my own limitations in Haiti. It was and remains exceedingly difficult to see a blue baby with a heart murmur in whom I suspect a septal defect (an opening in one of the walls of the chambers of the heart) and know that at home a simple echocardiogram test could yield the diagnostic data we would need to schedule relatively simple corrective surgery. In Haiti there is no access to cardiovascular surgery, much less pediatric heart surgery even for a simple thing like a ventricular septal defect. There is little hope of even getting an echocardiogram. And given that no intervention is available, one would need to ask of what use is the information anyway?

I have come to realize and accept that my skills are better used evaluating what basic population based health problems exist that I might be able to intervene with to make a difference in children's lives across the population. Given that all-cause mortality in children in Haiti is 30% before the age of 5 and that 15% of children die before their first birthday, mostly of preventable diseases, there is clearly much work to do.

An effective medical missionary will evaluate the needs of the indigenous people and the resources that exist with them and see how they can help with those instead of trying to fit their particular skill set into a system which most likely will not accommodate them. While I could use many specialties as examples, I will use my own situation to illustrate this. I could work long and hard to try to bring pediatric cardiovascular diagnostic tools and the facilities to do such surgery to Haiti. Perhaps that may be a worthy endeavor.

But in reality, it seems to me, my energies are better used in other ways. As I have observed the children I have seen in clinics across Haiti, I have concluded that what the children in Haiti need is clean water, vaccinations, adequate vitamin and mineral intake, maternal education regarding prenatal and postnatal care, and access to antibiotics for respiratory problems. Designing a comprehensive approach to even one of these factors with a limited population would consume the energy of even the most diligent and hard working medical missionary, yet with the right financial resources would be a relatively easy thing to do.

When I have evaluated what God's calling is for me and those I work with I keep coming back to the same thing—that cup of cold water. This translates into the following questions: *What basic needs are lacking here that I can work to provide which will positively affect the lives of the most people?* What is the cup of cold water that I need to prepare to give to these needy people given my own talents and resources which God has given me?

These are difficult questions and ones which are not easy to answer. We come from a land of plenty. Access to highly sophisticated and effective health care is widely available. So to change thinking patterns like this is difficult. In my US based clinic, 10% of the children I see there may have failure to thrive as a diagnosis for various reasons—the least of which is lack of access to food. In our clinic work, nearly 90% of the children we see exhibit moderate to severe malnutrition.

I would love to help the one or two blue babies I may see in a week long clinic there. But morally I am obligated to do what I can to change the situation for the 150 others who simply need more food. The blue baby most likely will die in Haiti. This is a hard fact to face but a true one. It is within my power to alter the futures of all those children who need more to eat or antibiotics for pneumonias to help them reach their fifth birthday.

I am not, in any way, advocating shunning or dehumanizing those we can't specifically help or those for whom we have no physical interventions. Quite the opposite. They need to be shown an extra measure of the compassion of the Christ we serve--as do their families. It is in these people that the real character of Christ will be manifest and we should be grateful for the opportunity to allow the Holy Spirit to work through us to them, as difficult as it may seem.

It borders on being immoral to use valuable financial, human and other resources to construct facilities or design programs which will provide services for a small select sub-group when such widespread basic needs exists within the population as a whole. I have seen this happen many times as good intentioned folks try to use the talent they have to help others.

My personal experience exemplifies this. Early in my work in Haiti, as I talked to the community leaders about what their perceived health care needs were, the first thing on their list was latrines. My initial response was—someone else who doesn't have my skills can do that—what else do you need? I can provide health care to you. What do you need for that?

However, as I thought about it, what I realized was that in this community of several thousand where no latrines existed, it seemed intuitive that having access to safe human waste disposal could only benefit them. Improper disposal of human waste exposes the population to diseases such as typhoid and intestinal parasites. Consequently, proper management of human waste in and of itself could improve the overall health of the community.

After that discussion with the community leaders, I came home, pulled up everything I could find about latrines and latrine construction on the internet to educated myself. Given this was such a basic and critical need in the third world, there was no need to reinvent the wheel. The World Health Organization, among many others, had designed and implemented a program called Vision 21 which incorporated sanitation (latrines) and hygiene education. Thus, the genesis of our community wide sanitation project was conceived.

This was not rocket science, nor was it pediatric cardiology. But it was a fundamental need of the community which they perceived (and I agreed) would potentially bring a positive impact to a large number of people within the community— including the children. It was the only place to start.

I pursued getting funding and to date more than half the latrines have been built by the local people. The Haitians are in charge of the design and construction. We discussed their design which was good and with what I learned through my research, I suggested one design change which would increase the effectiveness and longevity of the latrine.

The next phase will be a community wide basic hygiene program. Data shows that simply disposing of human waste does not alone decrease the number of waste borne diseases in a population. It must be linked with a hygiene education program. This will be a home based hygiene program and will be based on the Medical Ambassadors community health educators program. Agent Sante's (community health workers) will be taught basic hygiene and then will bring the information to individuals households as well as evaluate its effectiveness after a period of time.

Basic needs such as prenatal evaluation and careful clean cutting of the umbilical cord have already altered the infant morbidity and mortality in many communities in a way that free standing clinics with regular missionaries and mission teams may not. These are simple and easy interventions which can be done economically. The potential impact on the target population will likely be significant.

No--this isn't curing cancer in Haiti, or fixing kids congenital heart defects. Nor is it even rehabilitating amputees. These are all worthy and noble efforts in the right circumstances. But in an environment where there is 80% unemployment, tenant farmers cannot grow anywhere near what they need to just feed their families, where the life expectancy is 49 years and 30% of the children die before age 5 from preventable causes, it is clear where the most work needs to be done.

So instead of the analogy of thinking big, I would encourage us to think smaller-think of the less sophisticated needs-the cup of cold water. Think about latrines instead of bone marrow transplants. Think about clean water instead of bypass surgery. Think about tetanus prevention in newborns instead of laparoscopic surgery facilities.

As I have evaluated my talents and how I could use them to serve Him in your life, I asked God help me think out of the box. I looked at all my talents—my basic high school education for one thing. I had never been trained in how to build a latrine. But my education and access to resources allowed me to learn-and very quickly at that.

So for me, cleaning out a supply room that might allow us to be able to care for more patients, in my view of third world medicine seemed like a good use of my time at that moment. I felt pretty sure that others, who might have been asked to do the same thing, would not have been willing.

That being done, Eddy and I headed back to the other post op rooms to begin making rounds. In the first room, where the young boy was who was in pain the day before, I noticed that his bed was empty. I asked his mom where he was. She said that they had to take him back to surgery. The surgeon decided that his pain was caused from something that needed to be corrected surgically. He was getting it fixed even now. I was relieved. At least he would have his pain lessened.

I continued to make rounds on the patients that I had seen the day before. Since dressing changes were ordered every other day, most people didn't need those done. I busied myself with monitoring pain medication, IV fluids, and general nursing care. There seemed to be more nurses in this area than the day before.

127

More relief teams were getting into Port au Prince daily. That was a relief. When we came in that morning, I noticed a new Korean team which was now caring for patients in two of the four triage Zones in the courtyard alongside our team members.

As the morning progressed, it was hectic but only because of the amount of work that needed doing. There were no real emergencies or urgent things to care for in the post op area. I saw the woman with the two broken arms again. She was more comfortable today. I instructed her daughter in how to give her regular doses of over the counter pain medications and to come and get me if she needed "another shot".

I began to see things improving over the course of the day. Another group of new nursing staff had taken over the pre-op area. They were sorting the supplies out, making the equipment organized and useful to hold as many patient as the area could and allow them to work better. As more nurses were arriving, it seemed like the overall system was becoming more organized and functional.

While walking back to the pre-op area, one of our team doctors, Nandor, from Hungary, ran into me. He said he was working in the Intensive Care Unit and they really needed some help in there. He asked if I could come back and help.

Eddy and I followed him back. He introduced me to Kelly. She was a Haitian American nurse who seemed to be in charge. She said she could really use some help. None of their staff had had breaks since the evening before. So of course, I said I would help out.

HCH did not have an intensive care unit. Few hospitals in Haiti did. The ones that had what they might call intensive care units rarely had anything like the equipment that we might see in an ICU in the states. No cardiac monitors, ventilators, or specialized intravenous lines to measure heart function.

Kelly proved to be an exceptionally resourceful nurse who had transformed one of the unused operating rooms into a room where patients could get more observation and nursing care than those who were other places in the hospital. We had viewed the ICU on our initial tour and I did make a mental note that it was air conditioned. It was about 11 AM now and getting hotter by the hour. So being asked to help out there was something I was glad to do—for a lot of reasons.

Kelly was a Cracker Jack nurse and was clearly in charge. She spoke fluent Kreyol and was a great asset for that reason as well. It was clear she knew what she doing was so I just did what I was told. It took some of the pressure off of me. Her personality was such that she commanded respect almost immediately upon meeting her.

She told me her story in a brief moment when our attentions weren't on patients. She was from Miami but her parents had moved from Haiti to the US. She had traveled to Haiti often to visit their relatives and was familiar with the pre-earthquake in Haiti. She spoke fluent Kreyol because it was spoken often at home.

When she heard of the earthquake, she called her supervisor and said she had to go. She got a flight to the DR and travelled alone from the DR to Port au Prince. At that point, she just showed up at the hospital and began to work. After having spent the last two hours with this remarkable woman, I had no trouble at all believing this story.

There was one other nurse in the Intensive Care Unit, who, gratefully, left as soon as I arrived. Additionally Nandor was there. Kelly pointed me to a frail looking young woman in a bed near the wall. She said she needed to have a unit of blood hung. Her hemoglobin was 2.

129

Hemoglobin is a protein in the red blood cells that carries oxygen to the cells of your body. Additionally it helps to carry iron so it is necessary for energy and adequate breathing. Normal hemoglobin for a female is about 11-14 grams per deciliter of blood depending on the lab that is doing the blood test. Most Haitians are pretty anemic-have a low hemoglobin-due to poor nutrition. We often see hemoglobin's in the 7-9 gms/dl range in our clinics in Haiti. The average American would be pretty tired and short of breath with hemoglobin's in the 7-9 gms/dl range. But Haitians live with this on a daily basis. There is some adaptation but they are often short of breath and tired too. They just have no choice but to go on.

This woman's hemoglobin was 2 gms/dl. I must admit I have not ever seen a patient with hemoglobin that low. I have seen 4 gm/dl but never 2 gm/dl. It seemed to me to be the lowest that one could have and still be compatible with life. She didn't appear to be injured by the earthquake, just sick. I suspected she had malaria and a severe component of malnutrition. Malaria will destroy the red blood cells in the process of the illness. So both things could have been taking their toll simultaneously.

She looked like she weighed about 80 pounds. It is common to see very thin malnourished women in Haiti. They often sacrifice food to feed their children and the normal monthly cycles will also deplete their red blood cells if they are not replaced with adequate nutrition.

One way to tell how anemic a person is quickly without blood tests is to look at the area just beneath the lower eye lid. If you pull the lower eye lid down, the conjunctiva, the mucus membrane behind the lower lid, should be nice and pink or red. This is an easy way to tell if a person had adequate red blood cells. Often in our clinic work in Haiti, I will use this to gauge how anemic a person is when we don't have access to laboratory tests. I pulled this woman's lower eyelid down. You couldn't tell where the milky white of her eye ended and her even paler conjunctive began—it was that pale.

In the US when a nurse hangs blood there are very specific protocols to perform prior to giving blood in order to prevent giving a patient the wrong kind of blood which results in a serious reaction. It must be checked three times, the patient's armband must be matched to the code on the blood bag and the nurse must make sure the blood type is the same as what was in the chart.

Of course, carrying out much of that in this situation was pointless. We had no charts, no way to check to make sure that her blood was typed correctly and no other way to verify the blood supplier.

I asked Kelly, "What is you procedure for checking blood?"

She turned to me quickly and said "There isn't one. Check to make sure it is the patients name and just hang it."

In reality it was amazing we had access to blood at all. There were many patients who might have needed it following their surgeries but Haiti has no blood bank system in the same way we might think of it here. An occasional good hospital like Zanmi LaSante, in Cange or Albert Schweitzer might have blood. But also finding donors would be difficult as well. As you have heard earlier in this book, most people get donated blood from relatives.

I wasn't completely comfortable with the process, or lack thereof, that Kelly stated but what could I do. I did have Nandor check the bag to make sure it had the patients name on it. I verified the patient name with her and had another person ask her what he name was. So at least I made sure it was the person whose name was on the bag.

I asked Kelly if we had solumedrol, a steroid, to give in the event she had a reaction. She indicated that was available in the medications we had in the ICU. It is important to take a patients temperature before giving blood. A fever is one of the first signs of blood reaction.

The blood transfusion went pretty well. While that was going in, I checked on a couple of the other patients there. One was a young woman who had given birth the day before to a preemie baby-32 weeks. Both were doing OK but we wanted to make sure this new life and his mom had all the care we could give them.

Another patient was seriously ill. She was one of four patients I would see that week with tetanus. Although tetanus is often associated with rust, especially rusty nails, this concept is somewhat misleading. Objects that accumulate rust are often found outdoors, or in places that harbor anaerobic bacteria-bacteria that don't need oxygen to grow. But the rust itself does not cause tetanus. The rough surface of rusty metal or other object merely provides a prime habitat for tetanus bacteria to reside, and the nail or crumbling wall, in this case, affords a means to puncture skin and deliver bacteria into the resulting wound.

Another form of tetanus, neonatal tetanus, is common in Haiti, occurring in newborns who are delivered in unsanitary conditions, especially if the umbilical cord is not cut with a sterile instrument and becomes contaminated. In the United States, this is prevented not only by sterile delivery conditions but because immunizations are required and the immunity is passed from the mother to the newborn.

Patients with generalized tetanus present with lockjaw in 75% of cases. Other complaints include generalized stiffness, neck stiffness, difficulty swallowing, restlessness, and reflex spasms.

Later on generalized muscle rigidity becomes the major manifestation.

We had been told that immunizing all of the patients with wounds that we saw at HCH was imperative. However, we would see cases of tetanus throughout the week. Unfortunately, 2 of the 4 people who contacted clinical tetanus that I saw that week didn't survive.

The woman in the ICU that afternoon was quite seriously ill. She wasn't breathing on her own. There was a simple ventilator in this room and it was being used on her. She wasn't conscious. Patients with tetanus are given high doses of muscle relaxing drugs in order to relieve the muscle spasms. This results in them remaining unconscious. Her blood pressure and heart rate were stable so for that day we were just monitoring her.

Later this afternoon I walked by a room where an elderly quite sick looking man was calling out and no one seemed to hear him. I went in and immediately recognized him from yesterday. Yesterday he was lying on the ground in the hospital foyer covered up, but just barely, without any clothes on.

Next to him was a sign which was so eerie to me: "IV fluids only, DNR". This was what palliative or Hospice care looked like in the middle of the worst disaster in modern history. A cardboard sign sitting on the floor next to the patient...

He had sustained a spinal cord injury and there was really nothing to do for him. He had no family with him. Today he just wanted something to drink. It took me a minute to find a small medicine cup to use to give him water. He couldn't sit up. So I spent about 5 minutes just giving him sips of water.

I realized at that moment that it seemed to be the situation that Jesus described in Matthew 24 when He says we need to feed the hungry, give drink to the thirsty and help those in need. I was living that verse right then. Later on as I reflected on the day, it might have been the most important things I really did all day long.

I met up with Romel today. It was an emotional meeting. His family's house and he and Fregga's house are completely destroyed and they are living on the street. He was very discouraged about what the future holds. I reassured him we were going to be there to assist them in rebuilding their lives. These are people we know and who were affiliated with our ministry directly who we needed to be in a position to help once there was a system in place to do so.

Our team continued to be spread out throughout the hospital, paramedics doing triage, dressing changes, and other things. The two docs were manning the post op and ICU's with me and others. The other two nurses were at a different hospital helping out with many patients who had neurological and orthopedic injuries. All were representing NC Baptist Men well in this effort.

Half our team was staying the night to help relieve some of the night staff and will return in the AM. I got on the van to go back about 5:30 along with three other people. It had been a long day. We headed back to the compound.

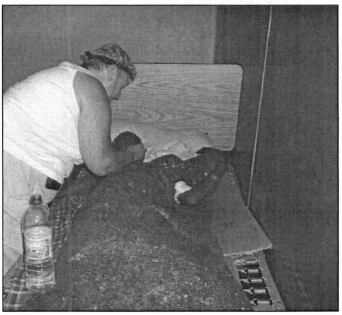

135

Chapter 10
The Watermelon Room

At supper on Friday night, I reviewed a bit of my day with the other two nurses on my team. They had been working with another surgical team that was staying at Global Outreach. The hospital where they were had many people as well and seemed similar to what we were encountering. I expressed to them that I still really wanted to help with kids if I could but at HCH there were only a couple of kids.

One of them looked at me and said "You should come over to our place. There is a whole floor of kids with no nurses upstairs. We are doing all we can to take care of the adults that come in through the ER."

I was really surprised to hear this since I had been expressing all week that I had pediatric experience and would be glad to help with kids. As we talked further, she told me that she had spent a few minutes in a palliative care unit where some children who were seriously ill and had no families were being cared for in the upstairs sections of the hospital.

The hospital-St. Damien's Ti Frere, Ti Sere (Little brothers, little sisters) Hospital-was a relatively new hospital, only 3 years old. They had a functional Emergency Department. Because of that, they were getting all kinds of injuries from the earthquake and had many adults as well. These surgeons were part of a team from Ohio who had been in Haiti for several days before we came. They had two surgeons, an anesthesiologist, a nurse anesthetist, and a registered nurse with them.

I expressed a desire to come over there the next day since there were no nurses and I did have pediatric experience. Later that evening, I spoke with the physician who was heading up the HCH team about it. He agreed my skills would be better used there since we had few children at HCH.

As I went to bed that evening, the implications of seeing how this terrible natural disaster had impacted the children of Haiti was an ominous thought, but I was glad that I could finally see my specific skills being put to use, especially since there was no relief team doing the post op care for over 100 children.

Before I went to bed, I texted this message to Shelia:

> *"They asked me to come to the pediatric hospital today. No one was there taking care of an entire floor of babies, orphaned and sick. Please pray this might be hard."*

The next morning it was just three nurses from our team that boarded the bus. The rest of the team had decided to stay to cover the night shift and were supposed to return in the morning to sleep. I met the new group I would be working with at St. Damien's. Phil Hurley was the main surgeon whom I would be working with. He was doing most of the surgery there. The other two doctors were traveling in with us but were working at a sister hospital of St. Damien's-Camillian Hospital, run by the order of St. Camillus-doing surgery there.

St. Damien's was located very close to the US Embassy in the center of Port au Prince. The area of the city is known as Tabarre. It is a relatively new hospital only 4 years old. St. Damien's is the only free pediatric hospital in Port au Prince. Run by Fr. Rich Frechette, a physician and priest, St Damien's mission is described best by Fr. Rick on his website:

"In Haiti, clean, beautiful facilities have never before been for the poor, those who live on the scraps and the trash discarded by the rich. For this reason specifically, St. Damien hospital is expertly landscaped with beautiful tropical blooms, the hospital is bright, sunny and breezy, and the maintenance staff work tirelessly to keep it clean. For our patrons, those who are used to receiving the scraps, there is a remarkable pride evident on their faces and in their posture when they step onto the grounds of St. Damien. Our mission is to not only treat the clinical ailments, but the spiritual condition as well. "

As we pulled up to the hospital, it looked much the same as HCH.   There were people all over the well manicured lawns and well landscaped circle drive. They had made their own tents similar to HCH. He was right in his description above-which I was to read several weeks later. The grounds were beautiful. Tropical trees and plants were well placed around the grounds and lined the drive way. The landscaping was well done. Several benches were located in various areas on the lawn. There was little evidence of damage to the hospital building and the surrounding structures.

There were also two very large canopies which extended from the front two walls of the hospital, hanging like giant awnings. Under these huge awnings were many patients placed in beds lined up in rows. The hospital lobby looked much like HCH, patients on every floor space that was available. Many different types of beds, from cardboard to cots, were present.

The hospital was much nicer inside because of its newness. Mary, my colleague, showed me to a room where they left their things and told me where I could come for the lunches which Global Outreach staff had packed for us. She also showed me where the water was kept. Then she pointed upstairs and said that was where the children's wards were.

I grabbed my backpack and headed up the stairs. This hospital was built like all of the others. Two square sections on each side of a central stairway provided the two wings of children's rooms. A large open air courtyard was located in the middle of each square section. St. Damien Hospital is affiliated with Nuestros Pequeños Hermanos, founded by American priest Father William Wasson. In addition to providing medical and surgical care, the organization runs a residence, camp activities, and school for orphans and other vulnerable children. It also distributes food and water to communities in need and provides vocational training opportunities. St. Damien Hospital is funded through private contributions and the support of Friends of the Orphans, Our Little Brothers and Sisters, and the Passionists, a Roman Catholic religious order. Under normal circumstances, St. Damien's has 120 beds for inpatients and the outpatient clinic saw about 100 children daily.

I didn't really have any guidance about where to go, so I just went into the first room at the top of the stairs. There was a middle aged woman in a lab coat in this room with about 15 children of all ages--most in cribs. She had a folder in her hand and was standing at the end of one of the cribs. I told her I was an advanced practice nurse with the America 1 team. Could I be of help to her?

She gave me a look of great relief. "Yes, this way", she said, and grabbed my arm as we exited the room and headed down the hallway.

She took me to a room on the far end of the wing. On the wall just outside the door, there was a metal sculpture of a watermelon slice with a small bite taken out of it. This was the Watermelon Room. All of the rooms were designated by these kinds of symbols-the Tap-Tap Room, the Sailboat Room, the Turtle Room, etc.

139

She told me that there was no one caring for the patients on this end of the hall. I could start in this room. The room was a good sized room and held 12 cribs and one regular hospital bed. The room was clean, newly painted with murals of animals and children's stories. It looked like a tropical open air version of a room one might see at Duke Hospital, where I worked. A desk was centrally located next to the door which had three chairs around it. There were two wall mounted revolving fans-one worked and the other didn't. The one which did work provided some air movement.

When I turned around, the Haitian pediatrician was gone. I guess I was on my own. There were two Haitian staff members who entered the room later. I found out one was a nurse; her name was Betty. The other was a Haitian nursing student, Tatiana. Since all of the schools were not functioning, many nursing students had showed up at the hospital wanting to volunteer their help.

I asked them if the patients had any records. Tatiana showed me to the desk in the center of the room. On the right hand side was a wire file holder which held the folders for each patient. This hospital was far more organized than HCH. They actually had some semblance of a patient chart assembled for each of the patients in the room. The charts were in a simple manila file folder but they held a sheet which gave the patient's name and all their demographics, a record of their evaluation in the Emergency room if they were seen there, and three other important pieces of paper. The first one was a medical progress notes sheet. This is where each provider would document the care they had given. The next was a medical order sheet. This is where the surgeons or other providers would write down the medical orders for the nursing staff so they would know how the doctor wanted the patient cared for. The last was a record sheet the nurses used to write down things like the patients vital signs, temperature, and other things of that nature.

This was a gold mine to me. To actually have something that resembled a patient's chart with useable and important information in it to me at this point in the trip, especially after what I had been working with for the last three days, was more wonderful than words could tell. It wasn't all a bed of roses though. While this would make my job so much easier, many of the charts were written in several languages which would take some time to decipher.

From first glance all the patients seemed to be stable, with no urgent needs. Several of these little ones had surgeries, most involved at least one amputation.

I began with the first patient, Revolus Angelois, an 18 month old who has sustained several injuries; an external head injury which had a large dressing on it, an injury which resulted in the amputation of his left lower leg and a broken right arm. His mom was with him. With Eddy there to help me translate, I began to ask her how things were going with him. She indicated that they would be coming to take him down to the surgery area to do a dressing change later today and for that reasons he was "NPO"-no food or drink by mouth. It was good she told me that because I didn't see it noted anywhere on the chart that I could decipher. I looked at the dressing on his head. It looked clean and dry. Since he was going to the OR to have his leg dressing changed later, I decided to wait to see if they changed this dressing also while he was under the sedation. That would save him any additional discomfort. He seemed to be doing OK. His mom said he didn't seem to have any pain.

I wrote my findings down on his chart in the appointed place on the medical progress note and went on to the next patient. Before I could get completely through his chart, I heard a loud scream from the other side of the room. It was a shrieking piercing scream loud enough to be heard all over the top floor of the hospital. The child was crying out for reasons unknown to me at that time. I dropped what I was doing and ran toward the sound of the screaming to see what was happening.

There, one of the Haitian nurses, who were floating through all of the rooms, had undressed a wound on a 10 year old female patient. She was pouring betadine-an iodine based antiseptic-directly on a large, gaping, open wound which measured about 6 inches across.

Cronise La Croix was a 10 year old girl who was lying in the only regular hospital bed in the room. She had sustained a serious wound to her foot from a falling wall, resulting in the removal of most of the skin on the top part of her foot, exposing the muscle underneath. This is called a "degloving injury"--named because it resembles what one might think would happen if a glove were the skin and one were to remove it as we remove gloves from our hands. The wound was very deep. She had also broken her ankle.

She was number 12 of the 12 patients in the room so I likely wouldn't have gotten to her until later in the morning. However, this crisis required my immediate attention. I screamed for the nurse to stop.

"Kampe! Kampe!" I yelled to her once I saw what was happening. "Stop! Stop!"

Cronise was screaming and crying loudly in pain, understandably. This was perfectly normal and expected-given the pain that would be inflicted when iodine is placed directly on an open wound.

"Kampe! Kampe!" I continued to yell as the nurse quickly turned around and saw me running over to her.

I tried to tell Eddy to tell her to stop immediately. She thought she was doing the right thing. Who knows how many other

142

times this child had suffered this kind of treatment from an unknowing but well intending Haitian nurse.

Just as I was trying to stop the procedure, another American nurse came running in the room. She too started talking loudly, questioning what was going on. I was quickly trying to explain that I had just arrived less than an hour before and had not been able to get to this child yet. She was also very upset as I was. She wanted to know why the child had not been seen by the American Orthopedic surgeon. I again tried to explain that I had just arrived as the only relief worker in this whole area and was trying to make my way around to see what needed to be done.

She quickly explained to me the procedure for getting one of the orthopods-a slang term for an orthopedic surgeon-to see the child. I told her I agreed with her and would take care of it immediately.

As she left, I went back to the Haitian nurse. Although I was very upset, I tried to explain to her calmly, that I didn't want them to do any further dressing changes until I had seen all of the patients. I told her that this was a very painful way to try to clean this wound and there was better way to do it. I must admit, my attempts at being calm and understanding with her were not very successful.

This was to be my first of many interactions with Haitian nurses where the way they worked with the children was less than desirable. Before I go further, I want to explain the role of the Haitian nurse in the Haitian health care system.

A Haitian nurse is not comparable to an American nurse on any level. The focus of the Haitian nursing care system is on the technical areas of nursing-dressing changes, starting and monitoring IV's, inserting catheters etc. Although they do receive training on pathophysiology and disease processes, much of this book knowledge is not translated into conceptual knowledge which would be used to formulate plans of care for a patient based upon their diagnosis.

My exposure to Haitian nurses has been on a limited basis. The hospital nurses I had observed in the hospitals around Haiti on my mission travels, had not been active participants in the care of patients as much as the person who delivers the medications, starts IV's and sits at the desk. The clinic nurses I had worked with had a range of skills depending on the venue where they were located. One particular nurse in the northern part of the country we had worked with had 15 years of experience and was quite skilled at diagnosing and treating many things in a way that would be comparable to US standards. On the other hand, another particular clinic nurse I worked with did little more than take blood pressures and do weights.

American nurses are highly skilled and sophisticated health care providers. They have extensive knowledge in normal functions of the body and how disease processes alter these. They are taught to problem solve and to plan care based upon the potential and actual problems that a patient may encounter with any disease. They are taught to think conceptually and less technically oriented. Although US nurses deal with a lot of highly technical devices and equipment, these devices give them information that is used to formulate a plan of care based upon the information obtained. Additionally US nurses are an integral part of the care team, for the most part; their input valued and listened to. They are responsible for recognizing changes in the patient's condition which would warrant notification of the physician or other health care provider. All of this takes a thorough and comprehensive education.

Haitian nurse have few of these responsibilities. They function more as health care technicians, "doing" things as opposed to seeing, understanding, thinking through, processing, and planning care of a patient.

That being said, the nurses in Haiti function fairly well at the level at which they are taught. But it would be frustrating and unfair to hold them to the standards one might hold of a US nurse. So a fundamental understanding of their role in this situation was essential in order to know how to most effectively use them.

I had hoped to develop a good working relationship with the Haitian nurses I encountered at this new hospital. However, I wasn't off to a very good start-screaming at the woman for what she was doing. However, my concern for the patient had to take precedence at that moment in time.

I asked her to step away from the bed for a moment and told Eddy to tell her I would talk to her in a moment. I returned to Cronise's side and tried to console her. She was alone, with no family members at her bedside at the moment. Her tears were flowing freely and her cries were loud. Understandably she was fearful of anyone coming around her now, but I used what Kreyol I had to tell her I wouldn't hurt her and that I was there to help. I told her that we wouldn't be doing anything else right now. As best I could, I tried to console her. She wouldn't let me touch her and pulled away. I tried to provide a presence that was calming and reassuring to her. One of the other moms with the child in the bed next door also came over and helped out. Her wound was still exposed and needed to be dressed at least before we were done.

Once I got her to stop crying, I went back to the nurse who was waiting at the desk with Eddy. I apologized for yelling at her but told her that it wasn't OK to cause that kind of pain in this child to change her dressing. I tried to explain that there were different solutions that she could use to clean the wound which wouldn't hurt.

I asked her if she had any hydrogen peroxide. She indicated that there was some on the shelf in the room. I went to the shelf she pointed at and located the bottle. I also grabbed a couple of dressing pads and some tape. My plan was to just lightly redress the wound enough to keep it covered and safe until I could get the orthopedic surgeon to look at it-which would be soon, I hoped.

As Eddy and I approached Cronise's bedside, she immediately started to cry out again. I asked Eddy to tell her that I wasn't going to hurt her again. But I needed to put a dressing on her foot. He knew what to say. That has been my experience with all of my medical translators. When a lengthy conversation has to take place or some kind of convincing needs to be done, I just give the translator the information and let them talk with the patient freely. They have a better understanding of how to approach them and can better address the specific issues of any particular conversation. I just stood there and waited until Eddy was done. She had agreed to let us try to put the dressings on.

Carefully and over the next 10 minutes I was able to place the two dressing pads on the wound and wrap it in gauze. Placing the final top one, I breathed a sigh of relief that we were done. When we finished, Cronise had a big smile on her face that I would come to look forward to over the next few days.

This whole event had taken nearly an hour. It was now 10:30 and I had only fully seen one patient and dealt on the surface with another. But it was clear that Cronise had to have an orthopedic surgeon look at her before we could decide what was further needed.

The Surgeon was Phil Hurley- a wonderful man and skilled doctor I would come to work closely with over the next few days. He was also staying at our compound and had been in the van with me that morning as we rode in. I took her chart downstairs and obtained directions as to where they were located. As I entered the room, he was in the middle of doing a small procedure-debriding a wound on another patient. I started to back out but he motioned me to come on in. I gave him a quick rundown on Cronise and told him I thought someone should see her today and at least evaluate what she needed. I felt she needed a skin graft and it was unclear if we had a plastic surgeon available. He said he would be up shortly and would look at her then.

Phil had a great bedside manner. His calmness immediately put me and everyone else in the room at ease. I was to see later just how skilled he was as a doctor. He and his team from Ohio had been in Haiti for a few days before we arrived so they had knowledge of how to get things done at St. Damien's.

I returned to the Watermelon room and began to see the rest of the patients. Getting through each chart took a bit of time because of the languages. The next patient was an 18 month old who was being cared for by the Italian team. He had an amputation of his right leg below the knee. His father was there with him. He was sitting up in the crib and seemed to be doing OK. His father also told me that his was going down to the OR today for a dressing change and was NPO-meaning her couldn't have anything to eat or drink before the surgical procedure. Again, I didn't locate that in the chart. This was important information for people to know. I was beginning to see one thing I needed to take care of quickly.

That was: SIGNS. There needed to be signs above each bed with important information which could be seen by health care providers quickly. This seemed to be the more humanitarian version of the "tape on the forehead" that we used at HCH. I tucked that thought into the back of my mind and continued to see the other patients:

Judelye Nans Debel- 2 years old with a high left leg amputation and a broken left arm in a cast up to his shoulder. Mom was at his side. He was doing well-going that day for a dressing change in the OR. Cared for by the Italian team

Peterson Louis-12 years old with a fractured left leg and large laceration (cut) on his right leg. The left leg was infected with gangrene by the time he arrived at the hospital and couldn't be saved resulting in a below-the-knee amputation. He was doing OK. No pain; eating and drinking OK.

Adeline Joseph-6 years old. Both femurs (thigh bones) broken and in a special kind of cast called a spika cast. Her left leg had been amputated below the knee. Mom was there.

Sophia Marcelus-a 9 year old with a large wound on her left leg. She was in the bed next to Cronise. The two seems to have developed a friendship. She was doing well with her Mom there.

Johanne Jean Baptist-9 years old. Closed head injury. Unconscious. Mother and grandmother at bedside.

Stevenson Pequidre-3½ year old with an amputation of his right leg below the knee. Doing well with his Dad taking care of him.

Pierre Jeanalson-a 4 year old boy with fractured right arm. Arm in a cast and Mom taking care of him.

The other three beds contained children who would come and go rather quickly over the next three days.

Except for one...

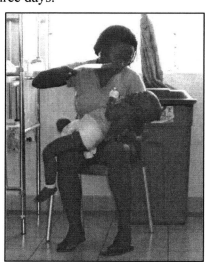

**Judelye
with his mother**

Chapter 11
<u>Angeline</u>

Each day brought with it its own challenges. As much as I would like to think that the day before would allow some of those challenges to be easier to deal with, new ones crop up almost every moment.

I reported to the Watermelon room when we arrived the next morning. Within the first three hours I had started three IV's, hung blood, received a patient who was having seizures and was on an IV infusion of Dilantin--strong anti seizure medication. I was beginning to feel like things were getting out of control.

I was hanging a blood transfusion on Adeline, the little girl with the two broken legs and spika cast. From the corner of my eye, I saw two young men come in with a young girl on a stretcher. We were never told when a new patient was to arrive. They just showed up. She was put in the one empty bed that I had. I hadn't really noticed her because I was concentrating on getting the blood in the IV running. It took several minutes for me to get to her but once I came within 20 feet of her bed space it was clear what the problem was.

The smell of gangrene is not one that you can forget. It was definitely there. I knew she had it before I even laid eyes on her. No one told me anything about her and there was only a short paragraph written on a paper that lay on the end of her bed from the makeshift ER. It stated that she was dropped off at the ER with no parents. They weren't able to get her complete name. Apparently someone had found her-now 12 days after the earthquake-and simply brought her to the ER. How she survived in the meantime is a miracle in itself.

An alias Haitian name was written on the top of the sheet. The Emergency room note stated that she had gangrene in her left leg and severe lacerations and wounds on her right leg and hip. The note indicated that they wanted and "ortho consult in the AM". That was written at 10 PM the night before with no signature and nothing else except that she had received two antibiotics.

It was now 1:00 PM-- the following day.

I quickly looked her over. I couldn't see all of the toes on her left foot because of her dressing but the ones I could see clearly were gangrenous. Her leg was bandaged up to her thigh; there was a large amount of drainage, which also smelled. Her right leg was heavily bandaged on her thigh. She also had heavy bandages on both of her legs and buttocks I estimated she was about 4 years old. She had an IV in which was running well. She wasn't fully awake but did arouse easily.

I knew this little girl had a very serious problem. I was concerned that no one in the ER had taken the initiative to see that someone from Ortho had seen her sooner. It was this kind of thing that I think had the potential to happen often—someone falling through the cracks. Likely the shift had changed after that note had been written, other patients had come in which took the attention of the staff away from Angeline for the night, and then when the morning group came on, they simple transferred her out of the ER because newer patients commanded their attention at that time.

Even though her condition was quite serious, it was easy to get lost in the shuffle—especially since she was alone and had no parent to advocate for her or at least keep her in the forefront of the relief worker's attention. She had gangrene that was at least into her foot and lower leg and from the smell likely was well up into her leg. She was now 12 days out from the injury and had had no care in that amount of time. She was dehydrated and

150

malnourished along with everything else. It was quite possible that the infection had spread to her blood stream making it life threatening.

Gangrene is a complication of cell death characterized by the decay of body tissues, which become black (and/or green) and malodorous. The smell of gangrene is very distinct. Once you have smelled it, you won't forget it.

We had to act fast to save her life and I knew it. I did a quick assessment, grabbed her chart and ran down to the special procedure room where Phil was working. I told him about the child. Sensing that it was serious, I told him I was going to send her for x-rays to see what was actually broken and then would return with the their results. But I wanted him to have a heads up about her. I thought she would need to go to the OR as soon as possible.

He agreed and told me to let him know when the x-rays were completed.

I stopped by the x-ray room on my way back upstairs. I needed to expedite getting her x-rays so she could get to the OR. This was my first experience with x-ray's at St. Damien's. I quickly found the lab from directions someone in the hall way gave me. The door was locked so I knocked. When the door opened I was surprised at what I saw.

First of all, I could feel the air bathing my skin like a cool shower. This room was air conditioned. What a relief-especially since I was now dripping with perspiration-it was mid day in Haiti-and I had been running around all over the hospital trying to get Angeline the care she needed.

The room contained a state of the art digital x-ray system. It had one x-ray table and x-ray machine. On the counter were two computer screens and a keyboard. These were used to order and display the x-rays. Digital x-rays are displayed directly on a computer screen instead of the x-ray films which are developed like film in a camera. Digital films can be magnified, rotated and edited in other ways to make viewing them much easier for the physicians doing it. I was really surprised to see this modern and very expensive piece of equipment in this hospital.

Fortunately the x-ray technician spoke English. I quickly told him the story-we had a seriously injured girl who needed plain films of her legs and pelvis before she went to surgery. It was an urgent case.

He was very helpful as he said could do her right away and would send a transporter up to the Watermelon room to get her. I quickly returned to the Watermelon room to get her ready. When I returned, I made sure her IV was working well and that she was continuing to respond when I aroused her.

Getting x-rays wasn't a problem but getting someone to take her there was. When 15 minutes had gone by and no transporter had arrived, I decided I couldn't wait any longer. She was oozing from all of her wounds. I found three of the absorbent underpads that we put on the beds under patients to protect the sheets. I had Eddy help me tuck them into my scrubs around my neck and waist. Donning a pair of gloves, wrapped her in the sheet which she was laying on. I grabbed her up in my arms and started out the door. I was going to take her to x-ray myself. I just couldn't wait any longer.

With Eddy holding her IV bag, we walked quickly down to x-ray. This wasn't an easy task. We had to maneuver down the stairs since there were no elevators. In my mind's eye, I felt like this looked like one of those scenes I had seen in medical shows or movies that I always think is ultra dramatic-and that rarely, if ever, represent reality in medical situations. But here I was, experiencing it in real life.

When we got to the x-ray room, the technician was waiting for us. He asked me to lay her on the table. At this point Angeline was whimpering quietly, likely in pain from the movement of the serious wounds on her tiny body-now 12 days old and filled with life threatening infection. He asked me what her name was so he could enter it in to the computer. I told him that we didn't know because she was alone. They had put a Haitian name down but it wasn't her own.

Over the next 5 minutes or so, this young man quietly and calmly worked with Angeline by speaking to her in her own language in a manner that allowed her to trust him. He comforted her and got her to tell him her name. Through his patient and calm approach, he came back to the control area and said she had told him her name. It was Angeline Pierre.

I was grateful for the moment to sit down and soak up some of the air conditioning while I had a chance. It was a blessing that I was conscious of. Even with the chaos and sense of urgency around me, I was able to notice the small things-a chance to stop and smell the roses in post earthquake Haiti-if there was such a thing.

It took about 15 minutes to do the x-rays. I was worried that she wouldn't lie still for them but she did. The technician was masterful at positioning her without causing her undue pain. I had never seen a Haitian trained x-ray technician. I never got this young man's name but his work is engraved in my mind-even now as I write these words-7 weeks after this experience. His compassion and skill literally gave us the information needed that would go on to save this little girl's life and he did it with such grace, poise and professionalism. He was one of the hero's of the disaster relief effort in my mind.

The great thing about digital x-rays is that they are ready immediately. The screen pans across digitally bringing each row of pixels up as they are transmitted to the machine immediately upon doing the x-ray. I watched as the x-ray picture was composed, row by row on the computer screen. Once the front view was completed, I couldn't see anything that obviously looked like a fracture of her legs. Her pelvis showed two definite gaps in the hip bone areas in the same place on both sides. On someone else, this might have indicated bilateral pelvic fractures. But on a four year old, I thought it likely indicated her growth plate-normal separation in the bones of small children which grow together over time.

As the second view of her legs and pelvis was coming up, I decided to run down to the special procedures room to tell Phil that the x-rays were ready for him to view. He was finishing up on a case and said he would be right down to look at them I told him that we had found out her real name. I wrote it down on a post it note and stuck it to the wall near where he was working so he could look her up in the computer system.

The x-ray viewing computers were located in a small room adjacent to the room where the x-rays were actually taken. Doctors would go into the viewing room, type in the patient's name and pull the x-rays up to view them right there on the screen. This same procedure was happening at the same time in multiple areas in the hospital where I worked at home-in the Unites States-even as it was here, in the middle of the worst natural disaster in modern history.

Eddy and I carried Angeline back upstairs to wait until Phil looked at the x-rays and decided what the rest of the day would hold for her. I placed her gently back in the bed. She was crying quietly again, the result of pain due to movement. I hadn't given her any pain medication at that point and decided she might benefit from some. I wanted to be cautious knowing she would soon be undergoing general anesthesia but I felt she still needed something to help with her pain.

Since this was the first day I was at St. Damien's, I hadn't had time to get my stock pile of supplies and equipment together. So I ran down to the pharmacy and asked for some IV morphine. What Potipar, the very able coordinator of the supply area, handed me would cause me alarm that continues to this day. The bottle of liquid morphine contained morphine at a concentration of 50 mg per milliliter-50 times stronger than what we have in the United States.

It would be hard enough to give an adult the dose they needed from this concentration much less the dose needed for a 4 year old child who weighed a fraction of what an adult weighed. I really couldn't believe what I was seeing.

It was hard for my mind to begin to think in the direction it would need to in order to figure out how to use this drug. I could use it all right, but it would take some calculating, diluting and then finding the right kind of syringe which would deliver the tiny amount that I would need to help Angeline without over-dosing her. My mind was already functioning in overdrive trying to prioritize, manage, be aware, assess, and care for all of these children. Now to have to do this complicated calculation would take mental energy and thought processes that I wasn't sure I had at that particular point in time. I really needed to sit down and think about what I was going to do. This could cause a serious problem if not handled correctly.

Fortunately, I didn't have to manage it right then. Phil quickly entered the Watermelon room. He told me that Angeline had the most serious form of gangrene-gas gangrene-and he needed to operate on her immediately.

Gas gangrene is a bacterial infection that produces gas within tissues. It is a deadly form of gangrene Infection spreads rapidly as the gases produced by bacteria expand and infiltrate healthy tissue in the vicinity. Because of its ability to quickly spread to surrounding tissues, gas gangrene is a medical emergency.

Phil told me he hoped he could save her life-he was fairly certain he could not save her leg.

He also didn't know what the wounds looked like on her backside and the back of her legs. They would have to be dealt with when she was asleep. He had already spoken to the OR staff and they would be ready for her in about 10 minutes when they finished setting up the room. He was headed down to the OR to scrub in and asked if I could get her down there in a few minutes.

Thankfully I didn't have to deal with the morphine issue at that point. Soon she would be under general anesthesia, feeling no pain at all, so it didn't seem to be that important and it would take critical minutes away from what I needed to do now-get her down to the OR.

I put a new IV bag up, regulated the rate and again prepared myself to carry her down to the OR. Wrapped in the underpads again, I grabbed her in my arms and with Eddy carrying her IV bag, for the second time in that hour; we headed downstairs to the operating room. Just as I was rounding the corner to the hall where the OR was, I saw Phil coming towards us. Our timing was perfect. The automatic doors to the OR opened and one of the OR technicians met us. He directed me to put her on the stretcher next to the door. And with that, we left her in the able hands of the OR staff.

Eddy and I walked back upstairs now, without the sense of urgency we had had for the last 90 minutes, since Angeline had arrived in my room; her diagnosis clear by the smell that surrounded her. If she had a chance to live, she was now in the place where it could happen. I breathed a quiet prayer to God that her gangrene wouldn't be so extensive that Phil couldn't save her. I asked for Him to guide Phil's hands and mind in order to care for her.

That was how most of my prayers were over the week. A quick thought prayer-"God, help me to do the right things". "God, give me a clear mind right now". "God, please help this individual get the care they need". And then I would get back to my work. Nevertheless, it was clear that they were heard and answered.

When we got back to the room, things were pretty stable. Eddy and I had a moment to sit down at the desk and get some water. It was the hottest part of the day. We were both drenched in sweat. I thought about taking a quick break again at the x-ray room. How wonderful that would have felt at that moment but I contented myself sitting across from the fan blowing right on my face.

I still had other patients to take care of, so we couldn't dawdle. Another young girl had come in earlier in the day. She wasn't injured from the earthquake. Her mother told the ER that she had a history of a seizure disorder. She had a seizure that morning and hadn't woken up from it in the time that she usually did. When she arrived in my room she had an IV running which had a label on it indicating it had Dilantin powerful anti-seizure drug, in it. Dilantin can be fatal when given through an IV if not monitored carefully. There was no machine controlling the rate and I had no idea how much of it she had. Since she wasn't seizing right now, I shut it off. It was dangerous to have it running when I couldn't control the rate it was going in at. In the United States, someone would get written up and likely suspended for this kind of action. But there were no machines that controlled the IV rates available. However, since I had no information, I just shut it off.

This child wasn't conscious and was breathing in a manner that people often do after having seizure -deep heaving snoring type breathing.

157

I noticed that the IV wasn't working well so that needed to be restarted. I wasn't really sure what we could do for her. I knew there wasn't a neurologist available at St. Damien's. So I tried to stabilize her and wait to see if she woke up. Since she wasn't a surgical patient, the Haitian pediatricians would be caring for her. The surgeons only took care of the patients they did surgery on. Since she had a medical problem—as opposed to a surgical problem--the Haitian medical staff would care for her.

When one of the Haitian pediatricians came in, I told them about her. I gave them a brief history of what I knew. Her condition hadn't changed in a couple of hours. The Haitian physician felt she needed to be transferred to one of the rooms on the other side of the upper floor where medical patients that were more seriously ill were being monitored from there. I was relieved that someone else was going to be responsible for her since there wasn't much to do except to watch her. The Haitian nurse, who was helped out occasionally, got her ready to be transferred by inserting a tube into her stomach, putting her on some oxygen and transporting her to the new room. I was grateful as I had had my hands full with the other patients.

In a couple of hours, Angeline, accompanied by Phil, was brought back to our room. She was alive but missing the lower part of her right leg. He told me that the gas gangrene had invaded most of her lower legs and he couldn't really save it. He felt the infection was localized to that area, which was a relief. She was now on IV antibiotic around the clock which would lessen her chance of the infection getting into her bloodstream. The wounds on her buttocks and back of her left leg were extensive and likely would need skin grafts but that was something that could wait until later.

When I went to check her after talking to him, I noticed that on the pristine clean dressing on her lower right leg which was now missing a foot-was written in large letters "America-1". That was how each team identified the patients they were following.

The Italian team did the same thing. It made it easy for us to know which team to contact when there was a problem. Personally I think they liked signing their work this way-it was a sense of surgical pride-at least for our team.

When I left a little after 5 PM, Angeline was still sleeping. She would wake up easily so I knew that this was the normal recovery process from general anesthesia but I didn't wake her very vigorously.

I really felt like I was looking at a miracle. A child, found 12 days after the earthquake in a lot where buildings had collapsed, with extremely serious injuries and infections was brought to the ER without parents and was now lying comfortably-yes without a lower right leg-but alive. She was almost lost in the system. A few more hours of not being noticed and the gangrene would have ravaged her body, making saving her life impossible. Even with that she wasn't out of the woods yet.

It had been an exhausting day.

At supper I was contemplating this part of my extremely complicated day when Phil came up to me, leaned over my shoulder and said "You do realize, April, that you saved that little girl's life today?"

I thanked him but said it was something we all did together and that she could still die of sepsis (a serious blood infection).

His response caused me to stop eating.

He said "No, you picked up that she needed attention NOW and brought her case to me with the forethought that we needed to act quickly. That was the turning point for her. Yes, she could die of sepsis, but I really believe she has a fighting chance".

I hadn't thought about the reality of it until he said it—just how fragile her life was and how close to the edge she had been. I guess I knew it back in some recess of my mind which was filing all of these experiences away. They were getting saved in my minds hard drive but weren't ready to print yet. There just wasn't time right now.

It wasn't until Phil spoke it out loud... and it was only then, at that point...... that I began to weep. What I had done was part of my training and it comes as second nature. I had acted and reacted without much thinking, thanks to my training and experience. And then it was filed away for later.

But when Phil said that, my mind began to quickly reflect on what might have happened if I had been MORE tired, MORE stressed, LESS concerned with what was going on and I might have missed this opportunity to save this child's life. That was the moment when the tears of relief flowed.

But I had acted quickly and acted well. Together we had saved a child's life who likely would have succumbed in a few hours. God was gracious—keeping Angeline alive until we could get to her. Now she had a fighting chance.

I reflected that as I was to go forward in this work, much of what I did was a result of our professional training and years of experience. It becomes second nature. One must think on one's feet in situations like this. I realized that this isn't a place for someone at the low end of the learning curve.

The huge responsibility of literally holding a life in one's hands became very apparent to me at that point in time. While I tried to have a good perspective that tragedies like this would be here long after I was gone, and many more would need to be helped, I still could do my part. It also drove home to me the point that I must continue to be as diligent as I could and not become complacent or distracted. People's lives were literally in the balance here and I was here to keep them from going over that edge as they lay so close to the precipice. But I also realized I couldn't fix it ALL.

For me, I realized, yet again, as I had so many other times in Haiti that it was only through the power of the Holy Spirit that I could do any of it. It certainly wasn't something I can do on my own.

It was an amazing experience for all of us.

And one I wouldn't likely forget…ever.

Angeline
January 28, 2010

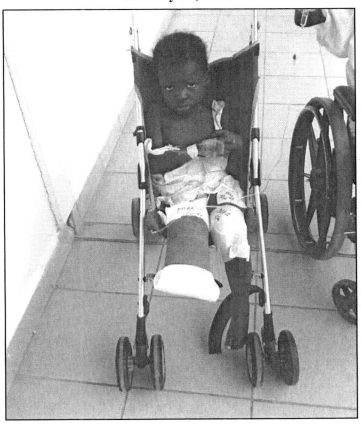

Chapter 12
<u>Cronise</u>

You are already familiar with Cronise, having heard of her before in this chronicle of God's love after the Haitian Earthquake. Cronise was the screaming child who was having her dressing changed. But her story deserves to be told on its own.

I met Cronise that morning when I stopped the Haitian nurse from using the iodine to clean her wound. She had not yet been evaluated by the orthopedic surgeons. Yet she had been in the hospital for 4 days before I arrived. I am not sure what the plan was for her except to just keep her there until she healed. That wouldn't have happened for a very long time-if at all. Again, she was someone who had fallen through the cracks-although her situation wasn't as critical as Angeline's.

Cronise had sustained her injury when the walls in her house had collapsed on her foot. Her ankle was broken and she had a deep wound on the top part of her foot which exposed the muscles deep down almost to the bone. She was alone when I first met her during that traumatic dressing change.

I allowed her to settle down and then let Phil know that he needed to see her sometime that day. It wasn't urgent but she needed evaluation. Since I had only a light dressing on her it shouldn't have been too difficult for him to see her wound.

He came up later that morning. With my help, and Eddy's, we convinced her to let him take the dressing off to look at it. He definitely felt it needed to be cleaned and debrided-removing of the dead and old tissue. He said they would be up to get her later in the day and that she shouldn't eat or drink anything from this point forward because she would need to be sedated for this procedure.

He asked me to talk to any relatives-if they came in-about what their wishes were. Then he left.

Cronise had a great smile and personality. Because she wasn't seriously injured such as to threaten her life, she had lots of energy, despite the fact that she had to stay in the bed. There were no wheelchairs available at the hospital so none of these kids had a chance to get out of their beds. She had taken up with the 8 year old next to her who also had a serious wound. She did have a father who came to visit her daily but for the most part the other mother tended to her needs that she couldn't tend to.

Once Cronise got over the pain from the initial attempt to clean her wound, her smile returned and that made me feel better. Phil had taken me downstairs after that incident and showed me what he had termed the "special procedures" room. This was a small room where a sterile environment could be maintained; a patient could receive some sedation by a nurse anesthetist on the team and get their wounds cleaned and debrided while not experiencing the pain that would come without the sedation. The reality was that on days before January 12, 2010, this "special procedures room" was actually some sort of waiting room for patients undergoing some other sort of procedure. It had a small bench in it, some cabinets and a place to sit. The sitting area now contained a procedure table which wasn't much more than the kind of exam table that you might encounter in a routine doctors office. But it was sufficient for a patient to lie down and have an IV pole hanging to administer the IV sedation.

Phil had said he would send someone up later in the day for Cronise. He would plan to clean and debride her wound under a light sedative in the special procedures room. I continued my work for the day and didn't think much about her until later in the afternoon when I saw Phil and David, the nurse anesthetist, come back in the Watermelon Room. He said things were just too busy down there and they weren't going to be able to do her in the special procedures room. Since it was a relatively simple procedure, he and David would do it right here in the room.

David made sure that her IV was working well since that was the vehicle through which she would get the medicines that would make her sleepy. It was. He told me he was going to use propofol, a very short acting hypnotic drug which means it causes sedation. Most people never heard of propofol until the last year. It has been mentioned many times in the news reports in connection with the death of Michael Jackson. The reason people have never heard of it before it that it is a very specific drug that is used under very specific circumstances-to begin anesthesia in the operating room and for procedures for sedation. Rarely is it used outside of the operating room. I personally have never seen it used outside of the OR. So when I heard that it might be connected to the death of Michael Jackson, I was quite surprised.

It is a good drug to use in situations like Cronise's because it wears off very quickly-usually in 30-60 minutes. This was important because we wanted to give her enough sedation to make her sleep but not to affect her breathing. If she was to be sedated more deeply she would need to have a tube put in her windpipe in order to maintain her airway and allow someone to assist her with breathing.

David talked to her calmly and told her that we would be giving her some sleeping medicine so she wouldn't feel any pain like she did in the morning. Cronise was still pretty scared and did begin whimpering. But within a few seconds of the medication going into her IV, she was sleeping soundly.

Phil asked me to get him some dressing material; saline to irrigate the wound and a table to work off of. We set up a little work table at the end of the bed near her foot. We didn't have the kind of irrigation solution bottles that I am accustomed to in the US. Ours have twist off tops like you find on a soda bottle. The ones in Haiti had a tab that needed to be pulled and my experience before had been that it often didn't open the bottle as needed. I had struggled earlier in the day with this problem.

As we got ready, Phil told me that she could heal without a skin graft but it would be a long and arduous process and not likely to happen in this environment. He reminded me that God made our bodies to heal themselves from problems like this long before there were plastic surgeons or skin grafts. That being said, he told me that if there was a plastic surgeon around, she certainly could use their help now.

He put on his sterile gloves and began to wash the wound with a surgical scrub brush. These are small square brushes that have an antiseptic solution embedded into them so that when mixed with water, they serve to clean anything they are being used on. As he began to clean the wound thoroughly, Cronise began to move around a bit. Phil stopped while David gave her a little bit more medication. This worked within a few seconds and she was quiet again.

He continued to scrub and clean the dead tissue off the wound. When it came time to rinse it, he also had trouble getting the top off the bottle of irrigation solution. The bottle was about the size of a 2 liter bottle of soda.

After working and working to get the top off, he finally just stopped and said "Well there is more than one way to skin a cat", after which he pulled a pocket knife out of his pocket, unfolded the blade and proceeded to cut the top completely off of the bottle.

He poured the solution over the wound to clean it for the last time and then dressed it. He pulled out his pen and marked on it

165

'America 1", the standard signature for our team, to allow those caring for her to know which team to call in case of a problem. The whole things took about 10 minutes. David had stopped giving her any additional medication. After a few more minutes she began to stir. For the next 20 minutes or so, Phil wrote his note while David monitored her as she began to wake up.

Once Cronise was awake and responding well, they left. Phil reminded me to see if there was a plastic surgeon around and if possible, to try to get her seen. They both waved as they scurried out the door. On to the next case.

Cronise was completely awake by the time the beans came around for the late afternoon meal. Her smile was back and she was laughing and talking with her friend in the next bed.

As I left the hospital that evening to catch the bus home, I looked on the sign-in sheet on the door of the team room. All of the medical care providers were to sign in on this large sheet of paper posted on the door so we could see exactly who was there and what resources were available. I noticed that a plastic surgeon had signed in just that day. It indicated he would be there for 4 days.

Note to self-"Find the plastic surgeon first thing in the morning and get him to consult on Cronise". So many details to attend to but this one was really important. I knew I would remember.

The next morning, I went directly to the team room where the computers were. I had brought my own laptop. But the Internet reception wasn't very good at the compound so I had starting writing my updates in a word document the night before so that they would be all ready once I was able to get a connection at the hospital. I wouldn't have to waste the precious time that I was able to connect with the Internet on actually composing the message. Once I got to my hotmail account, I just cut and pasted the message from the word document into the hotmail message

166

and hit Send. Usually I was able to get a connection long enough for that to be successful.

As I walked into the team room I checked the sign in sheet again. The plastic surgeon's name was still there so I asked the Logistics Officer how to find him. He told me what his cell phone number was. I wrote it down and went upstairs to the Watermelon room. Once I got my things put away, I dialed his cell phone number. I told him about Cronise and that I would like for him to consult on her case today, if possible, since he was only here for a few days. I was sure she could benefit from a skin graft. I gave him her location in the Watermelon Room and he assured me he would be up later to see her.

Later that day, a young plastic surgeon came in to the room and asked to see Cronise. I am sorry I didn't remember his name especially. But that was the only time I was to see him. He asked me to help remove Cronise's dressing. She trusted me now so she knew I would be careful and not hurt her. Once he saw the wound, he explained to me that he didn't have any dermatomes with him so he would have to use donor sites for the graft.

A dermatome is a surgical instrument used to produce thin slices of skin from a donor area, in order to use them for making skin grafts. One of its main applications is for reconstituting skin areas damaged by trauma.

There are two kinds of skin grafts-full thickness skin grafts and split thickness skin grafts.   The choice between full and split-thickness skin grafting depends on wound condition, location, and size, as well as aesthetic considerations.

A split-thickness skin graft (STSG) is a skin graft including the epidermis (the very top layer of skin) or the underlying and part of the dermis. A dermatome is needed to do a split thickness skin grafting. Its thickness depends on the donor site and the needs of

167

the patient. After being harvested with a dermatome, a split-thickness skin graft can be processed through a machine similar to a pasta roller machine which allows it to expand up to nine times its size. Split-thickness grafts are frequently used as they can cover large areas and the rate of rejection is low. Another advantage to the split thickness skin graft is that you can take from the same donor site again in 6 weeks. So if additional grafts are needed, there are donor areas ready to use.

Cronise needed a large graft but because there was no dermatome available, he would need to use full thickness grafts from a couple of sites. These would require additional time to heal and likely more post operative pain in the sites where the grafted skin would be harvested from.

The surgeon told me he had put her on the schedule for the next day. I made a note of it in the chart. I also noted it on the newly made signs I had put above each of the patients beds which gave important information quickly to those caring for them. She was to be NPO-nothing by mouth-after midnight for the surgery the next day.

Her father came in later that day and I explained to him what had happened. I told him that she would be getting her skin graft from a specialized surgeon from the US and that this would help her injury heal normally. He was very happy to hear that.

The next day about mid morning, they came for Cronise. Her surgery lasted about one and a half hours. She came back with a heavy dressing on her foot and two other dressings, one on each of her groins, where they took the skin for the skin graft. She was crying and said that her legs hurt-meaning the graft sites. I gave her some pain medicine which helped and she went back off to sleep. Everything looked great and the note in her chart indicated that the surgery had gone well without any complications.

The surgeon came up later that day. He said she needed to have the dressing remain in place for two weeks in order to promote the healing that was needed for the graft to take. Infection is a serious and common complication of skin grafts. Given that we were in less than ideal circumstances, I wanted to make sure she had every chance she could have for this graft to take.

So I wrote in large letters on her dressing in both English and Kreyol: DO NOT REMOVE BEFORE FEBRUARY 1/PA CHANGE APRES FEBRUARY 1. It covered the entire dressing and couldn't be missed by anyone caring for her.

Cronise's father came in later that day and was very happy to see that she had a successful surgery. She was fully awake and was her normal jovial self with her big smile blazing for all to see.

Although this part of the story is sad enough and while there is a good ending to it, there is a much sadder part to Cronise's story that hasn't been told.

She was one of 7 people in her family. Her mother and father had 5 children. Her father-one of the lucky ones-was employed by the government in the Ministry of Justice doing a non skilled job there. The Ministry of Justice was completely destroyed in the earthquake on January 12, 2010. But that wasn't all that was destroyed in their family that day. Cronise's mother and all of her siblings-5 members of her family of 7-were all killed in the earthquake. She and her father were the only remaining people in their family. Cronise was seriously injured; her father didn't sustain any physical injuries. But it was clear how devastated he was at the loss of the rest of his family.

On the day of her surgery which was the last day I would see her, he brought in pictures of his family to show me. I took a beautiful picture of her sitting on the side of her bed with her father, her arm resting on his shoulder, her newly dressed and marked skin graft the only visible reminder of the terrible tragedy which befell their family, except for the three pictures he held up to his chest-one of his wife and two of his other children. It was a stunning picture, like one you might see in Newsweek or Time. A family in ruins but a family that survived.

Cronise's wound could very well have been overlooked had our team not been there. None of the Haitian staff would have sought out a surgeon to clean and evaluate it. None would have looked around for the plastic surgeon that was only there for four days. Cronise would have just sat there enduring the agony of terribly painful betadine irrigations by the Haitian nursing staff. I am sure she would have had to rely only upon the God given healing powers of her body that Phil referenced to me the day before. Maybe her body would have healed itself, likely not. Under the best of circumstances, she would have healed with a terribly deforming scar which would likely have limited her mobility in her foot.

But she now had a chance. That was all I really could ask for in these horrific circumstances--that people just have a chance. Dermatome or not, she was able to get a skin graft and likely a good one.

I don't know what her outcome was, but I have very good reasons to believe that she healed up just fine, (as long as no one bothered that dressing), and that she was able to go home with her father to begin the life that they would now have in the devastating aftermath of this tragedy. She had a chance and I was privileged to be part of that chance. Me, Phil, and the plastic surgeon whose name I will never know. We all were the hands of Christ to her. He had no others but ours...

170

Cronise and her father, holding pictures of their family who were killed in the earthquake

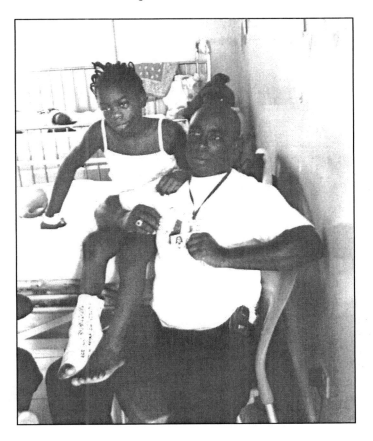

Chapter 13
Peterson

I saw Peterson the first day I arrived at St. Damien's. He occupied the bed back in the corner of the right hand side of the room. Initially I didn't pay much attention to him on that first day because he was sitting up in the crib, watching every move I made-a sign to me that he didn't have any immediate needs and as such could wait until I dealt with some other things first.

As time went by, I reflected that he might have felt that way a lot. I also noticed that there was no specific adult with him. He was sandwiched between an eighteen month old whose mother held him most of the time and Adeline, a 6 year old with casts on what remained of both her legs. Both moms had their hands full. Being situated in the corner between the two of them, Peterson mostly just sat in the middle of this activity and watched.

Peterson was 12 years old. We were told he had been brought to the hospital from an orphanage. I don't know where it was or who brought him but I never saw anyone there with him the entire time I was at St. Damien's. Peterson had a fractured left leg and large laceration (cut) on his right leg. The left leg was infected with gangrene by the time he arrived at the hospital and couldn't be saved, resulting in a below-the-knee amputation. When I first saw him, he had dressings on the front of his right leg and a dressing on the stump of his left leg below his knee.

Peterson was a quiet child, never really bothering anyone or making a fuss. He had his surgery early after the earthquake and was healing up well. So most of the days he spent sitting on the side of the crib that was his bed. All of the beds in the rooms were the regular hospital type cribs-high small beds with metal bar side rails that pulled up to prevent children from getting out of them. You can imagine how hard it must have been for this 12 year old to be in one of those. Although the side rail was down all the time, he still quietly sat on the side of the bed most of the day. When I first saw him he was dressed only in a tee shirt, a bit too large for him, and nothing else. He had a water bottle that he kept in his bed to urinate in. One of the mothers located around him would empty it when it got full.

Peterson did not require much care. Most of his wounds were healing nicely. I changed his dressing every other day without any problem. I was touched as I saw the mothers nearby assisting him to the bathroom when he had to have a bowel movement. They helped with bathing him and made sure he got his plate of food when the food arrived.

Something about this quiet child touched me. He never asked for anything. But seeing his leg, now half gone and non functional, while he sat in his bed alone, moved me in a way that other, seemingly more serious things, had not.

Later that morning, as I was rounding and talking to Peterson, he asked me it there were any other shirts that he could wear. He said his skin was itching from this shirt. When I checked with the mom's around me, they said he had been wearing it since he had arrived 8 days ago. I asked the Haitian nurse if they had any hospital gowns or anything else that he could wear. Not surprisingly, she said "no". Of course, it itched him. He had been wearing it for 8 days. I knew it wouldn't be easy to find something else for him to wear but it would have to wait until tomorrow because I already had an idea in my mind.

That evening, I let my team members know what happened with Peterson; that he was a orphan in the hospital with no one there caring for him and about how he worn the same shirt for 8 days and had nothing else to wear. I encouraged them to look in their suitcases, as I would that evening, and see if they had a tee shirt or two they could spare. I knew someone who could really use them. I asked them to lay them on my bed if they had any. It seemed ludicrous that in the middle of such a disaster, anyone would cling to something as irrelevant as a tee shirt when that was something that another needed greatly. Multiple tee shirts were placed on my bed that evening.

The next morning, I returned to St. Damien's with the tee shirts in hand. I went over to Peterson, along with Eddy, and told him that I had some new clothes for him. I showed him the tee shirts and his smile brightened up immediately. We quickly changed him into one. He grinned from ear to ear as we placed the other ones in a place where they would be safe. I showed them to the two moms who were helping him so they could change them as he needed it.

It was my second day at St. Damien's--late in the afternoon. I had about 45 minutes before we were to rendezvous at the bus to leave for the Mission Compound. Most of my work for that day was behind me. The day before I had noticed that a couple of the transporters had been using an umbrella stroller that they had found somewhere to transport children back to our room. When they brought the last child up there, the stroller was left behind I had finished all of the urgent work for the day and while sitting at the desk finishing up some paperwork, I noticed that umbrella stroller out of the corner of my eye. At the same time I noticed Peterson.

On an impulse, I grabbed the stroller and took it over to his bed.

"Eske ou vle ale ak sa?" I asked him in Kreyol. "Do you want to go outside in this?"

His eyes brightened up like fireworks and the biggest smile broke through on his face like a ray of sun through clouds on a rainy, dreary day.

"Wi", he said to me. "Yes."

I knew the stroller would be a bit too small for him but it was better than nothing. So I helped him down out of the high crib into the stroller.

I got him situated and he really did fit pretty well into the stroller. He had not been out of that room in over a week since he had returned from surgery. I knew it would make him happy just to be able to go outside.

I began pushing him and out the door we went. The top floor was designed in a square around a beautiful garden located on the first floor. Rooms with other patients in them outlined the square. We circled the top floor a couple of times and then I asked him if he wanted to just sit out here while I finished up. He said "yes".

I left him in the stroller sitting by the railing just looking out and waving to the people who walked by. He still had that bright smile on his face. I can see it in my mind's eye even now as I write this.

I left that evening and he was still sitting in the stroller. I asked one of the mom's if they would be sure to bring him in when he was ready and they assured me they would.

I left that day knowing these hands had made a difference in this little boy's life, not by any particular medical care I gave, but by seeing the need of the child who had been trapped in that hospital bed for days on end and just longed to be outside again.

The next day was my last day at St. Damien's. When I arrived, I saw the stroller still in the room in the corner. Apparently several moms had taken their kids for rides in it throughout the evening when Peterson was ready to come in.

175

Late in the morning, after I got things in order for the day, I went over to Peterson's bed and asked him if he wanted to go for a ride again. I must admit that I was beginning to feel the stress of the intensity of the work that I had been doing over the last 8 days. I had worked diligently in the direst circumstances, struggling to use the resources we had at hand to save people's lives, keep them out of pain, and promote their healing. I had no time to really "spend" with the patients in a way that would help ease their emotional pain or bring comfort to them. It seemed like taking Peterson for a ride again would help me feel that I had been able to do that-some of the most precious work that I value as a nurse. When I asked him, his face lit up with the smile and he nodded yes.

I helped him get in the stroller, now sporting his new clean shirt. We headed out the door and started around the top floor concourse. We couldn't talk very much. I speak some Kreyol but it is hard for me to understand people unless they speak slowly for me. Peterson spoke very softly so it was even more difficult to understand him. As we rounded the second corner of the square, there was a large room that held about 20 beds for patients seen the day before. But I noticed that there were only a few people in there now and they were cleaning out the space for some reason. My natural curiosity got to me and I stuck my head in the room to see what was going on. Much of the equipment was gone from the room but my eyes immediately focused on what I saw over in the corner. It was a bright red children's wheelchair. I know that it wasn't there the day before because I had looked for one. The only one I could find was in the parking lot out front with a bunch of other broken equipment. It was also broken-one of the wheels was not working so it wouldn't roll.

I was elated. This was just what Peterson needed!

"Peterson, we sa", I said. "Peterson, look at this!" And pointed to the wheel chair.

We rolled over to it. It looked like it worked. I tested it out around the room and sure enough, it seemed fine.

"Eske ou vle ale nan sa?" I asked. "Do you want to go in this?"

He nodded, excitedly.

I lifted him into the new chair. After a few demonstrations about how to roll the wheels with his hands, we took off out of the room and balcony hallway. I let him go down the straight part of the walkway and when he got to the corner, I just watched as he tried to figure out how to make the corner. With minimal demonstrating, he learned to hold the left wheel and roll the right when he wanted to turn left and to do the opposite when turning right. Suffice it to say by the time we got back to our Watermelon Room, he needed no further instruction from me.

What a gift I had found. I have no idea where that wheelchair came from. I know it wasn't there the day before and I know others had been looking for wheelchairs as well. I also know that God had done more amazing things than to make a wheelchair show up when an injured lonely child in Haiti needs one.

I was able to continue on with my other work because Peterson was able to be on his own now. He spent the entire rest of the day outside on the balcony, riding around and before the hour was out, he had become a real expert in the maneuvering of the wheelchair.

As other relief workers would walk by him, they would high-five him or make some salutatory comment to him to which he would respond with that big grin which would brighten anyone's day. The smile on his face as he rounded the corner coming down the walkway towards our Watermelon Room, wheeling himself in that wheelchair is one I will never forget.

Later that day, the first physical therapist to come to St. Damien's came into our room. She was just assessing all the patients and beginning to get them started on some muscle strengthening exercises. She was from the US but had lived in Haiti for the last 6 months working at St. Damien's.

She didn't have the right size crutches for Peterson. He was larger than the children's ones that she had and too small for the adult ones. So she tried to use a walker with him just to see how he would do standing on his one good leg. Because he hadn't used his good leg much in the last 10 days, it was very weak and he had lots of trouble supporting himself on it, especially with a walker that was too big for him. She got an idea of what he needed in the way of rehabilitative services and promised me she would work with him to get him on his feet with crutches but in the meantime, he could still use the wheelchair for his "social visits" outside.

On the last day I was at St. Damien I took Angelina out in the umbrella stroller to sit in the hallway with him-two orphan causalities--but survivors of this horrendous disaster. Angelia still had an IV; she had just returned from surgery the day before to revise her stump. I wanted one last picture of them. I parked the stroller next to Peterson's wheelchair and asked him to hold her IV bag up. The photo is one of the two of them sitting there side by side, in their various forms of transportation--each one missing a leg--Peterson his left, Angelina her right--both with other injuries—obvious victims, but survivors. When I returned home and looked over my pictures, I found that this picture, of all the hundreds that I took, symbolized to me the devastation of the event more than any other, and the hope of it as well.

So much so, that you will find it on the cover of this book.

April and Peterson, January 28, 2010

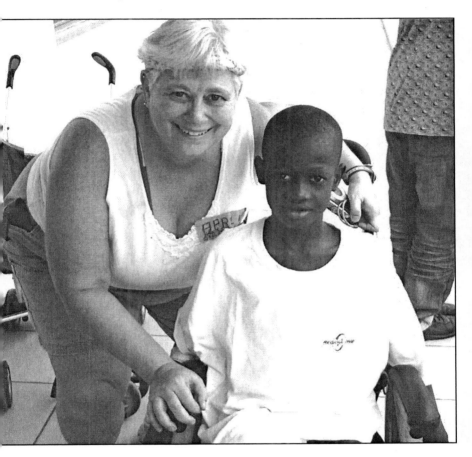

Chapter 14
Johanne

My first day at St. Damien's, it became clear to me that there were two types of patients here.

The first, surgical--those who needed surgery to repair traumatic injuries which they had sustained as a result of something falling on top of them, or some other trauma related to the earthquake. Examples of these kinds of injuries were broken bones, cuts or lacerations, and gangrene-most of the time requiring the treatment of amputation to save the person's life.

The second type of patients were the medical patients--those who had sustained injuries for which surgical interventions would be fruitless or not needed, and those who needed to be treated with medical therapy, such as medications and other treatments. The most common examples of these kinds of injuries were spinal cord trauma/injury and head injuries.

For many traumatic injuries where surgery is not an option, the prognosis tends to be more serious. Surgery is intended to "fix" things-make things workable, useable, and/or functional again. Medical therapy has to rely on the body's own innate abilities to heal or not, while using supportive medications or therapies, waiting to see if that is possible.

I learned quickly, after entering the Watermelon Room on my first day, that Johanne was in the second group of patients-a medical patient. There was no surgical team following her. That first day, before I went to round on her, I read her chart quickly. From the description there, I had an idea of what I was to encounter.　Johanne had sustained, in medical terminology, a closed head injury.　This indicated that her head sustained some trauma but no injury occurred to anything on the outside of her head-no lacerations or cuts on her scalp, nothing that could be seen from the outside.　But it was clear she had a head injury.

The dysfunctionality of the brain can be determined in many ways.　Of course, here in the US, that is best done through the use of a diagnostic test which actually shows a picture of some sort of the brain.　This could be in the form of a CAT scan or an MRI.　Both of these types of diagnostic tests provide the health care provider with pictures of the brain taken in thin slices so that you can see cross sections of the brain, identifying areas where injury has occurred.

If you know the reason for the brain dysfunction it is easier to determine what to do to try to correct the problem.　For example, if someone experiences a hemorrhage in their brain from defective blood vessels which break, that is treated differently from someone who has experienced trauma to the outside of their head causing swelling within the brain or the membranes that surround the brain.　This second type of injury essentially causes the brain to swell and be compressed inside the skull. Because there is nowhere for extra fluid inside the skull to go, as the fluid builds up it causes further compression of the brain. Compression of the brain results in the brain not functioning normally. This dysfunction will be exhibited in various signs which are detectable in a patient's behavior, motor skills or ability to think and process.

Johanne had sustained a closed head injury. As I walked towards her bed with her chart in my hand, her mother stood up expectantly.

"Eske ou we docteur jodi'a?" I asked her.　"Have you seen a doctor today?"

"Non", her mother replied. "No."

Just from a cursory look, it was clear to me that Johanne was very ill. She didn't seem to be awake at all; she had a tube inserted through her nose which went into her stomach. This was being used to give her medications. I noticed immediately a serious, troubling sign. Her hands and arms were both turned inwardly towards her chest instead of laying flat next to her as one might expect. This neurologic sign is called decorticate posturing.

Posturing is an involuntary flexion or extension of the arms and legs, indicating severe brain injury. Decorticate posturing means the legs or arms are turned inwardly towards the chest. In nursing school, I remembered this because I associated decorticate with the "core" or the body-decorticate/core. Decerebrate posturing, the more serious of the two, occurs when the arms or legs turn outwardly away from the body.

Johanne exhibited obvious decorticate posturing. I knew without any imaging or diagnostic studies that her brain was swelling and likely damaged to a significant degree. All this I knew without even touching her.

I asked her mother what happened. She told me that a wall had fallen on her. They had rescued her by removing the concrete that had trapped her but she was unconscious when they got to her. She didn't have any injuries outside on her body but she had never awakened. She told me she hadn't spoken or eaten since that time.

I did a complete neurological exam on Johanne. I checked her reflexes all of which were hyperactive- this was abnormal. She didn't respond to painful stimuli or to voice/calling of her name. She wouldn't move anything voluntarily. Her pupils were fixed and dilated. They didn't respond at all to light shining in them. This was the most serious sign. Pupils should normally contract when a light is shined directly in the eye. Pupils not responding this way indicated serious dysfunction of the brain-possibly critical damage.

I knew before I did any exam that she was injured seriously, likely fatally. Although I couldn't see specifically what was going on inside her tiny skull, I knew the tell tale signs of intracranial swelling--swelling of the brain inside of the skull. All of these things held a very grave prognosis for her-- especially since it had now been 10 days and she had had no treatment of any kind.

When the brain swells inside the skull, the lower portion of the brain, the brainstem-the location of all the very critical portions of the brain which control the breathing and other vital functions of life-are pushed through the tiny opening that leads from the brain to the spinal cord. This process is called cerebral herniation. Herniation is a deadly result of increased pressure in the brain and skull. I felt sure that, Johanne would eventually develop herniation due to the trauma her head had suffered. She had all of the signs.

The only way to prevent herniation is to treat the increased pressure in the brain. This takes sophisticated monitoring devices which are placed in the brain to monitor the pressure as medications are given to lower the pressure. There was just no consideration do doing any of this in the midst of this disaster situation.

The reasons were simple and obvious. First of all, it there were no physicians in the hospital who could attempt this. There were few, if any, relief internists in Haiti at that time. Most of the relief doctors there were surgeons. Additionally, these procedures require specialized nurses to care for the patient during the process of monitoring and medicating. There certainly were no Haitian nurses who could do this and the relief nurses were needed elsewhere.

Johanne's mother kept stressing that she hadn't spoken since they arrived. I have seen this in other families in the States who had had to deal with serious neurological situations, as well. They find it hard to accept that the brain is injured, most of the time irreparably, so that normal functions like speaking, waking up, eating, moving on their own just cannot occur. It is impossible because the part of the brain that controls them has been damaged and/or destroyed. Brain tissue does not regenerate, at least not in adults, so there is little hope to regain functions like this if herniation has occurred.

I examined Johanne thoroughly-more thoroughly than any of the other patients. I wanted her mom to know that I truly was concerned about her even though I knew her prognosis was grim. I asked her if she had changed any since she had been in the hospital-now 8 days. She said no, nothing had changed.

She was very concerned that she hadn't eaten in that period of time. Of course, her mom was concerned that she would never get better without eating. However, there was no way to feed her. She couldn't eat normally and there was no tube feeding available to feed her through a tube-if that was even something that would have been considered.

Obviously it wasn't.

Cases like Johannes's are routine in Haiti. Not in the specific problem she came to us with. But in the recognition that the resources are limited and there are often things for which we have nothing to offer. Recognizing our limitations is a daily task in Haitian medical care-at least it had been for me.

Don't take me wrong. I don't give up on a patient like this. I just realize that it will take something beyond my power or anything I have to give to change the situation. I tried to explain to her mom that she was injured very severely. And that I just didn't know when, or if, she would get any better. I told her I would try to see if there was a neurologist with the other relief workers and if so, I would try to get him/her to come and look at her. But I couldn't promise anything.

In my heart of hearts, I knew no neurologist would say anything different to her but at least I would help her to feel that her daughter had had every chance there was to try to get better.

I did instruct Johanne's mom in some exercises that would help prevent her arms and legs from getting stiff and contractured. She seemed happy to know that she could actually do something for her besides bath and clean her.

I checked the board downstairs when I went on my next supply run but there was no neurologist listed as being in the hospital. There wasn't even an internist or a medical doctor (as opposed to a surgeon). I felt like it was a long shot that I would be able to locate one but I wanted to keep trying.

Each day I went in to check Johanne, I did a full neurological exam. I didn't expect anything to change but I wanted to make sure I didn't miss something subtle. I am sure I spent more time looking her over than any other patient. I didn't want her mom to feel that she was being abandoned. On the second day I asked her if I could pray with her for Johanne. She said yes. Eddy translated while we stood over her beloved child, now living in the vale between life and the next life. I asked God for mercy for her and to please heal her in one form or another. Her mom seemed grateful.

On the next to last day I was at St. Damien's, I went to see Johanne in the morning. I noticed a picture taped to the top bars of her crib. It was a woman and a child. I realized immediately what it was. Johanne's mom had brought in a picture of what Johanne looked like before the earthquake. She was really unrecognizable from the child that lay before me. I knew it was her mom in the photo with her but the child in this bed bore no

185

resemblance to the child in the photo. This child in the bed seemed to have lost all life in her.

I asked her mom if the girl in the picture this was Johanne. She said yes and seemed quite proud to show me what she looked like. I took special time to admire the photo and thanked her so much for sharing it with me. I continued to encourage her to do the exercises and told her that after my exam nothing had seemed to change, for the better or worse. I told her I had been unsuccessful in locating a specialist to see her but would continue to try. She again expressed her heartfelt gratitude.

Throughout the time in the hospital, Johanne's mom never left her side. Her grandmother, who looked to be about 45 or so, came in regularly to stand vigil with her as well. I spoke to both of them as often as I could. Johanne's mom also helped to take care of Cronise since her father wasn't there too often.

I remember looking over one time and seeing a very poignant scene. Johanne's grandmother was sitting beside her bed in a chair. She was holding her hand and had her head lying on the bed, grabbing some rest for herself while she could. The devotion of both her mother and grandmother to Johanne was admirable and inspiring. I was able to snap a quick photo without waking her. It is one of the pictures that move me the most when I see it.

On my last day at St. Damien's, I made a special point to go to Johanne's mom and tell her good-bye. I wanted her to know that I would be praying for her and Johanne as I returned to the US. We had a final prayer together and I left.

Unless God intervened, I would expect that Johanne will be with the Lord at the time of this writing. Even if she were to be able to live with her severe mental incapacitation, the fact that she could not be fed would lead to her ultimate demise. My heart was saddened deeply by seeing Johanne and her situation. Johanne's world changed forever on January 12. The child in the photo on the bed likely would never return. Life for Johanne's family changed forever that day as well, as it did for hundreds of thousands of other Haitians.

I can only pray that the Lord will surround her family with the peace that only He can provide them.

Johanne January 25, 2010

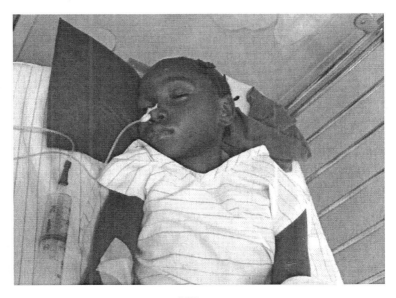

Chapter 15
...so much love 4U...

I had been so focused on everything I was experiencing, thinking so clearly about the images that were in front of me, the work that I was doing, the people around me, that I had little perception of what must have been going on at home.

I knew the people who cared about me and the work I was doing were surely praying for me. I was certain that there were prayers going up for me at all times of the day—and night. I was that confident in those faithful servants who shared my corner of the world at home. While the knowledge of their prayers would have been enough, there were other times when I got a very special blessing from their specific actions.

I had been sending daily updates back when I could but I had not been able to really read any messages I might have received through my email. I did have my new Blackberry® with me but the reception in Haiti was still so sporadic that I couldn't get access to the Internet through it on a regular basis.

But there were two times that the Lord allowed me to gain the encouragement that I needed, at the specific moments I needed them, through His servants and their responses to my emails.

On Thursday morning of our first week (the third day) I was traveling to the hospital n the van with my other team members. It had been a particularly difficult morning already. There were some conflicts in the team. I felt that people were beginning to show signs of stress in their ability or inability to cope with what we had seen. We had been there for three days now and it seemed like the initial ability to shut things out might have been deteriorating some. The realization of what was happening and individuals' ability to cope, or not cope, with that was affecting the way we related to each other.

I had a particularly difficult encounter with the team leader related to taking some supplies that the team members had brought with us from the States to the hospital. He didn't want to take them because it would inconvenience us in the way we had to sit in the van. I couldn't understand this reasoning or perspective when we were dealing with people who had had their homes collapse around them. Angry words were exchanged. I put the supplies on the van anyway.

I didn't speak on the way to the hospital. There was clear tension in the air. About 15 minutes into the ride, I felt a buzzing on my blackberry indicating I had a new message. I didn't always get these messages because the reception was so sporadic but this morning, I looked at the screen and saw it was a message from Shelia at home.

> *"just saying hi. many here send love. so much love 4U @aumc . hugs for you, prayers 4U. had this open this AM... checks. for Haiti coming in too, big and small. Also the new part of grace is OK. Only old hosp. is destroyed. They are seeing people per Baz.*
> *God is watching over you. he will be with you and touch every person you see. news shows the people cheering for usa as they see our military and others working so hard to help them. love to you.*
> *your sis Shelie*

"so much love 4U at aumc..."

Aldersgate United Methodist Church was my home church in Durham. It was Thursday morning so I knew she had been to the

Wednesday night prayer service the evening before. I knew that was what she was talking about.

"so much love 4U at aumc..."

What a blessing it was for me to read that simple text message at this particularly difficult time-especially since I was feeling so "unloved" at that moment. This statement was particularly significant to me because I was relatively new at this church. I had made the very difficult decision about nine months before to leave a church I had attended for 22 years. I had found Aldersgate to be a church which embraced me, my talents, skills, and desire to serve the Lord as His mandate instructed us. More importantly they were already serving the poor and needy in many, many ways.

I nearly wept when I read that text message. I knew that at home there were people who loved and cared deeply for what I was doing on their behalf because they couldn't-for whatever reason-do it themselves. They were praying for me, hugging Shelia in my stead, loving me from afar. That message sustained me through the rest of that difficult day. When we got to the hospital, the team leader and I went our separate ways. He was going to stay overnight so that gave us even more distance to allow the hard feelings to dissipate. I treasured that love from AUMC in my heart as I did the Lord's work with the injured in Haiti on that Thursday. I wrote Shelia back later in the day and told her just what that message had meant to me and why. The day had been difficult from the start. But the knowledge that there were so many back home who were supporting me with their prayers sustained me throughout the difficulties.

There was another time that God used the power of technology to encourage me during my relief work in Haiti. I was at St. Damien's hospital and was working very hard with Angeline when she first came in. You have read her story earlier in this book. What I didn't tell you in detail was that on that morning I

190

had three very sick children in my room—all who needed care at the same time. One had come in from the ER with a seizure disorder and another one had come in with respiratory problems and needed immediate attention. Trying to juggle these three really sick children was challenging and exhausting. About 2:00 in the afternoon, I had just sat down for the first time that day when I felt the vibration in my Blackberry® indicating I had a text message waiting on my email. The reception was so sporadic I usually didn't even notice this when it happened. But this time I did. I was sitting down so I decided to check it. I saw it was from a woman who went to a previous church I had attended. I knew she was on the list to get the email updates that I sent.

I noticed the subject line-"praying for you". Since it seemed like I was getting reception at this particular moment, I decided to open the message. This is what it said:

> *"April...I have been keeping up with you via the Luke's Mission website. I just wanted you to know that I am praying for you. NOW. Judy"*

I was overcome. Tears flooded my eyes. I knew that at that particular moment in time, someone was raising me up to the Lord. I was free to rest in the assurance that His Holy Spirit would hold me in His arms and help me do what needed to be done-despite the seemingly overwhelming circumstances.

I felt like I had just read a message from the Lord himself. Judy had been "Jesus with skin on" for me at that moment when things were especially difficult. And she was praying for me...NOW.

I made it through the rest of the afternoon but I was ready to leave when the van pulled up. It had been a very difficult, draining day. How much more drained would I have felt it there had not been so much love surrounding me, so much prayer going up to the Heavenly Father for me, so much care and concern about what I was doing there?

I will tell you that those small things sustained me during extraordinarily difficult times. I say that so that those reading this will know that there is nothing too small to give someone encouragement. No prayer that you breathe between one task and another that doesn't go heavenward and is heard and answered. When the Holy Spirit puts someone on your heart, heed His call. You may never know the difficulties that your faithfulness will help bring them through.

After I finished with everyone I had about 45 minutes until the ride came. So I went to the palliative care ward for the infants and spent some time there helping to feed the babies and change them. All of these children had no parents and are severely malnourished. I saw a 10 month old who weighed 5 lbs. That isn't all that unusual for Haiti considering 30% of the children here die before age 5 years old. I saw one little one that I was afraid to pick up he was so tiny-it was all he could do to eat. All of these kids had no parents before the earthquake and the only attention they got was from those who cared for them here in this ward. Two had parents before "the event" but they are orphans now.

Somehow feeding those little babies helped feed my soul that day.

I ran into these beautiful nuns that day, too. They were part of the Angel Ministries. They worked in an area near the earth quake and came here to see if they could help. They were just going around to each of the room where there wasn't a presence with the babies and holding them and talking to them. They were amazing women. They were easy to spot as they were in bright lime green shirts. I took a full video interview of them and you can see it on our website. Their presence made me happier that day.

Sr. Josephine from Angel Ministries at St. Damien's Hospital

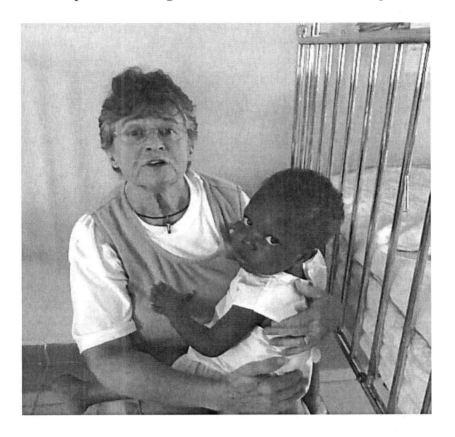

Chapter 16
"We lost everything…"
The Trip to Fondwa

Earlier in the week, I had talked with Eddy about the possibility of taking a day off from the work at the hospital and going to Fondwa to see how things were going with Sr. Carmelle and Sr. Simone. We had received very little word since the mission team which was trapped in Fondwa came home. But from their information, it seemed like they had been affected pretty significantly. I wanted to lend my moral support to the nuns. So in order to do so, I had brought a little bit of money that I could leave with them should they need it.

One of the people from Hungary who was traveling with our team was a reporter, Andros. We had a rough start to our relationship. Before our plane even landed in the Dominican Republic he made it very clear that he was very upset at what he had heard other press reports about the lag time in getting supplies in, administrative and bureaucratic hold ups in help and other logistic problems. It seemed like he had a bias from which he was going to be reporting. Within a few minutes of meeting him, I immediately disliked him and his attitude. However, over the course of the week, the sights and sounds we would experience would soften his heart and attitude and we actually enjoyed spending a bit of time together.

I told him that I was planning to go to a rural mountain village where there was an orphanage on Monday. My understanding was that they had taken a significant hit from the earthquake and I asked him if he was interested in going with me to report this story. Andros had relied on me several other times during the week to assist him in understanding things and their relationship to the culture and earthquake. So when I told him this might be a good story, he jumped at it and said of course he would go.

Eddy had made arrangements for us to take a private van up the mountain to Fondwa. It usually

costs about $100 per day to rent a vehicle and driver in Haiti. I knew it might be more now because gas was in very short supply. And I also knew people would be looking for work as well. Eddy was able to procure a vehicle for the day for $240. That is high under normal circumstances but it seemed like it was reasonable given the situation now. Besides, I needed to get there.

Andros and I rode the van to the hospital which was where Eddy and our driver were to meet us. I grabbed a case of bottled water for us, knowing we wouldn't be able to stop at any of the places where we normally stop for drinks on the way up. Everything was closed and nothing was getting in by way of new goods and supplies to the small stores that are located along the rural routes. I was not sure what would be needed so I really had nothing else with me except what was in my backpack.

We started off. It was the height of the traffic hour in Port au Prince at 8:30 in the morning. The earthquake had made little, if any, noticeable difference in the traffic, which is extremely congested at any time during workdays. Although the Haitians may not look like it the eyes of a foreigner, they are very safe drivers. They are very used to the congestion and lack of any obvious regulations related to driving and right of ways. You rarely see an accident in Haiti. Besides their skill at driving, there are also no freeways or high speed highways. Most of the roads where you could actually get up a bit of speed are too windy or dusty to allow you to do that. As a result of this, they rarely are driving fast-another reason that there are fewer accidents.

We started off on the road out of the city. Fondwa is a small village located about 30 miles up in the mountains above Port au Prince. It usually takes about 90 minutes to get there. The roads are good but very windy and all uphill, making traveling fast difficult.

However, the road out of the city is a different story. One must traverse through Carrefour (pronounced Car-foo), a very busy suburb of Port au Prince lying on the northern coastline. The traffic there is known notoriously for its congestion at any time of day. The roads are terrible. If there has been any rain at all, there will be very large areas of standing water mid wheel deep on most vehicles. It is hot, smoggy, dirty, and busy.

This was the first time I had been out in the city at all other than the roads we took back and forth to the hospital. I had really only seen a small part of the city. Although what I had previously seen was difficult, the worst was yet to come- I just didn't realize it at the time.

When we got to Carrefour, what I noticed immediately was what I have come to call, Median Tent Cities. Carrefour has a divided road-two lanes on each side with a small concrete median strip about 6 feet wide down the middle. As we got to this area of the city, I noticed that the median strip was completely filled with shanties made from bed sheets, strips of tin, wooden branches and most anything else one could find to put together a makeshift shelter. Each shelter was the width of the median strip. Each one had a common wall with the shelter next to it- thereby conserving resources.

This went on for over a mile and a half–shelter after shelter in the median strip of the road.

There was no other place to find shelter. Many of the buildings resembled the "concrete stack of pancakes" I described earlier- several floors collapsed on top of each other looking like a stack of pancakes. The rest were rendered uninhabitable due to the large amount of damage they had sustained in the earthquake.

After a week of seeing what I had been seeing as a result of this natural disaster, I still had a hard time believing things like this-people literally living in the streets.

Andros noticed this at the same time I did and we both got our video cameras out to shoot it. It is the kind of thing that is hard to show the full effect in a still photo. Cars were rushing by and people were sitting on the curb outside their sheet shanties in the median strip. The traffic was terrible. I was concerned because we had very limited time. I had to be back at 5:00 PM to catch the van back to the compound.

I sat stunned for the next few minutes as we exited the city proper and began the trek into the Haitian countryside. The ride was quiet most of the rest of the way. Andros was in the back seat of the van working on his video story which he would send back the next day. Eddy was conversing with the driver in Kreyol and I wasn't paying close enough attention to understand or really care what they were talking about.

Leogane is a small city that is outside of Port au Prince on the way to Fondwa. We had visited there many times and driven through it often. There is a small hospital there-Hopital St Croix. We had worked some there within the past years. I had actually stayed at the guest house there several times. Leogane was at the epicenter of the earthquake. It was described on the news as being 90% destroyed. We had heard that the hospital had sustained severe damage and wasn't operational.

As we neared the outskirts, I saw many of the small concrete houses were completed destroyed—now lying in ruins--piles of concrete rubble. Many people were just sitting beside these piles of rubble not really doing anything--just sitting there. Some had made makeshift structures of pieces of branches and tin or bed

197

sheets, but most had nothing. As we entered the "business" section of Leogane, I began to see that for once the news media wasn't exaggerating.

There was little left standing. Piles of rubble abounded everywhere. The whole back side of the hospital was gone, leaving a gaping hole which resembled a huge open wound. Many windows were broken. Doors were off their frames. The streets were just barely passable.

It is at Leogane that we make the turn to head up the mountain. At this point, I was speechless. I pulled out my computer which I had brought with me and began writing down some of my thoughts. Each day I had been blogging and sending it back to the States as I had opportunity.

Near the bottom of the mountain, the roads were pretty good. But as we began to climb the mountain, there were huge cracks in the road everywhere. Most of them were small enough for us to drive over. But in several places, the cracks were big enough to cause an upheaval in the road of several inches, necessitating that we drive around them in order to avoid damaging the car.

Additionally as we climbed the mountain, there were many places where one whole side of the road was covered with a mud or dirt slide, requiring that we navigate the road on just one lane, being careful of oncoming traffic on the other side. Some of these areas were caused by boulders which blocked one lane of the road. These increased in number and frequency the closer we got to the top of the mountain where Fondwa is located.

A trip that normally takes about 90 minutes took us over three hours. It was now nearing noon. We had to start back no later than 1:30 in order to get back to the hospital by 5:00 PM. The traffic in Carrefour is far worse at the end of the day than even what we had experienced in the morning. We had to allow for more time.

198

We arrived at the road which leads down to the village. It is very steep. I have traversed it many times--on foot, in a truck, and on motorcycles. This last option is a relatively new one. Some innovative young men started a small business of transporting people and things up and down the mountain road on their motor bikes for a small fee. I would much rather travel this way. While I never minded the walk-it is about 2 miles-because it is so steep, going down is as hard as coming up.

Eddy helped procure the riders for the three of us. Andros had never ridden on a motorcycle so it was a real adventure for him. We started out with the two guys on one bike with a rider and I was on another. But half way down, they stopped and dropped Eddy off. They would return to get him once Andros was dropped off.

As we got near the bottom of the valley, I began to see some of the damage that we had heard about. The small building that served as a storage area had collapsed. I saw that the guest house had also collapsed. Parts of some other buildings used by members of the community were also severely damaged. The road near the guest house, which was now dirt, had only one lane passable.

I got off the motor bike and asked a small child who was nearby, where Sr. Carmelle was. He pointed to an area next to what once was the guest house. That area had once been a beautiful garden which Sr. Carmelle had taken great pride in. I climbed the small hill and followed the trail to the garden area. What I saw took my breath away.

Many small children were congregating in an area which was obviously where they were staying. There were a number of multi-colored sheets and blankets swinging in the breeze, as they attempted to make a covering for a large area that had been cleared. Anything that was considered to be of possible use that was salvageable from the rubble was lined up along the edge of

the living area. A barrier had been made of some tin sheets which had been salvaged from houses that had collapsed. Old and wet mattresses lined the edge of this area as well.
There were three chairs and two benches placed in various areas around the clearing. Children milled around, a few of them playing quietly, but there was not the amount of activity one would expect from 50 children.

Sr. Carmelle walked out from under one of the coverings, carrying a small child on her hip, to greet me. The stress that this event had taken on her was immediately apparent to me. She looked completely exhausted. The normally bright shining smile which exuded from her peaceful face wasn't there. She put the child down and came over to give me a hug.
"Sister", she said-her term of endearment and nickname for me-as she reached her arms out to embrace me.

My eyes were already filled to overflowing with tears of sorrow. I couldn't stop them. This was the worst thing I had seen--50 children and 12 nuns living in this place of squalor. I had more to learn which would only serve to deepen my sorrow.

I told her I had very limited time because I needed to get back to the city. She was grateful I had found any time to come see her.

She took me over to an area under one of the sheets which protected us temporarily from the sun. There were two chairs there. Next to them were three mattresses laying on the ground. On one was one of the novices who had broken her leg. She had a cast from her ankle to her hip and was dressed in a night gown. Several young children lay face down on the other mattresses napping. Nearby was a small metal table on which sat a pot containing some beans and rice. Periodically someone would come up and take a small portion of it as we talked.

I asked her if I could videotape us talking so I could bring her story back to the people of the US and try to get them some help. She agreed readily.

Sitting with a two year old in her lap, she began to tell me what had happened. What she said broke my heart as I listened, the tears streaming down my face:

"The school is broken and the church is broken and the house for the church is broken. We have some neighbors, their house isn't broken but they are afraid to sleep there. They live here now (motioning to the clearing where we sat), everybody lives here now."

"We have about 4 people with broken legs and Sini from the school has two broken legs. We have about three people from the construction site of the school-they died all of them. And we buried about 4-one of them a Sister-Oudel-from this house"

At this point, her tears joined mine. She pushed her glasses up and wiped her eyes with her sleeve.

"And our beloved Jude..."

Her tears wouldn't stop now for a minute or so. Sr. Carmelle loved Jude so much. We had seen that just 6 weeks ago when we had visited Fondwa for a regular visit. It was the first time we had met Jude and the two were inseparable.

"And our love, Jude..."
At this point, the toddler nestled close to her chest is asleep, where he remained for the rest of the time I was there as she continued to talk to me.

"The Sister's house is broken—all of it. We lost everything," she said, as she motions with her hand to the areas around the clearing where we sat."

"And everything passed." she continued.

Trying now to regain her composure she goes on.

"But thank God we are alive, you know. Thank God we are here. But I am afraid to give the water to the children. There is so much death around here and there are much winds, so many people died," she says as she holds out to us a bottle of water.

"I was in Port au Prince and bought some of this water but it didn't last very long."

"We have problem now. We have a big problem to start back. I don't know if I will be here to see us get back. Something we took 20 years to build is gone in one hour," she said, her voice breaking now.

The strong stalwart of the community, the glue that holds this community together, is outwardly struggling and understandably so. My heart felt like it would explode out of my chest.

"We are very sad. But we aren't too sad for the broken house or the lost objects or the things. We are sad for the people who died."

She stopped there, needing to take a break. I took the camera and panned around the area, getting views of the people lying on the ground, the sheets blowing in the wind, the few meager belonging laying on the ground, the three pairs of children's shoes, the torn pieces of foam leaning against the tin fence, the single pillow laying in a small chair-- things that seemed so precious now.

She continued to tell me how she didn't have any medicine or anything she could use to treat people's injuries. Their food was sparse. She was able to go to the city once or twice a week and get a little bit of food.

Andros asked her a few questions about how the children were managing. He wanted to know what they planned to do about the damage to the orphanage. She didn't know at all. She went on to say that she had not been in Fondwa when the actual earthquake hit but had been in Leogane. It was clear that she felt like if she had been there perhaps Oudel and Jude might not have died. What a burden to carry.

I saw the time ticking away. I had about 10 more minutes. I asked her what she wanted me to tell people at home about this situation.

She said, "Tell them we need help. There are children here. We have no food and water. We have nothing now. I am afraid people have forgotten us."

I promised her I would take that message back. At the same time I reassured her that people had not forgotten her. I showed her on my blackberry phone a message from one of her sponsoring organization which said that they were trying very hard to get help to them from the army and aid agencies. She seemed a little consoled after reading that.

The time came to leave and it took every ounce of will power I had to make that trek to the car. I wanted so much to stay and just be a presence with her if nothing else.

I told her that I would send Sonel back tomorrow on his motorcycle. I had some water filters that I could give her which would make any water drinkable. She wouldn't have to worry at all about giving the children water from this filter. I also told her I would send back to them a bag of medical supplies and any food I could acquire. I told her I would send the motorcycle cabbies back with the rest of the case of water we had in the van. We didn't need it and they truly did.

When I asked her how she would survive, she just said "Well, we are here."

I prayed with her before I left but I have to tell you, it wasn't really a heartfelt one. It just seemed like all I could do.

It didn't seem like much, but it was all I could do at the moment and I thought it might help a little. The bike ride up to the top of the mountain was difficult for me as my mind struggled to leave my beloved friend in this unimaginable situation. 50 children and 12 nuns living like that-and I felt so powerless to do anything to help her.

We were already late. We loaded our stuff into the van, sent the cyclists back with the water and headed off back down the mountain.

I began my blog for that day in the car:

> ***Tuesday, January 26, 2010***
> *Today I went with a driver and a translator to the rural mountain village where my two close friends Sister Carmelle and Simone live and work. We had word that the village had been nearly destroyed by the earthquake and I really wanted to see them just to tell them how much I loved them and see what I could do to help first hand.*
>
> *I think this might be the most shocking thing to me that I have seen so far. I found the two of them along with 50 children from the orphanage they run and 7 novice nuns all living in a shanty constructed of clothes and sheets supported by some ropes on the trees. There were three tattered mattresses on the ground and a few chairs scattered about.*
>
> *The mission guest house was completely destroyed as was the sister's house and the adjacent small house for*

the novices. The orphanage is not safe for the children to live in.

As I talked with Sr. Carmelle and she relayed the events of last Tuesday. We both were in tears the whole time. She regrets not physically being there when it happened- she was in a town about 10 miles away on her way back- and thinks that perhaps the deaths might not have occurred had she been. She said what they needed most now was a tent some air mattresses and a clean water source. She is afraid to give the children the water they have. They are managing with meager portions of food that they purchase when she goes into a neighboring town. It was the most horrendous site I have seen so far. They have no sanitation. They all use one bucket and empty it twice a day in the woods around the complex.

There is no help for them in site. Although many people love and care about them, to get help to them now seems difficult at best. They are a two hour drive from the city and in a very remote location. When I asked her how she would survive, she just said "Well we are here". Pictures attached. They say more than any words I can add.

Under His crushing mercy,
April

Driving home I was heartbroken. I was struggling with myself to think if there was anything I could do to help her. I knew I would send some supplies up and whatever money I had left-it wasn't much, maybe about $300, but I would send it all. I didn't need any of it.

As we entered the city, the road we would normally have taken was blocked so our driver took another way. Before long we found ourselves right in the middle of the downtown area where the epicenter had hit. Again I couldn't believe it. We were driving in the area hardest hit by the earthquake.

Eddy said to me "Being in this area will make you cry. This is where most of the people died"

It was easy to see why.

The area looked like a war zone. There were few standing buildings for blocks on end. In usually Haiti fashion, there were no roadblocks cordoning off the area for people or vehicles. People were walking everywhere, near buildings that were barely standing. The more we drove, the more uneasy I became. It was clear that none of these buildings were stable and they could collapse at any moment. There was block after block of devastation for as far as the eye could see.

But even in the midst of this desolation there was a small market in operation. Four or five multi colored umbrellas had been set up in the middle of a street surrounded by rubble. A man was standing right next to the corner of a building that had a huge crack in the column which was supporting the whole side of the building.

Life just went on in Haiti.

I wanted to get out of there soon because it was clearly unsafe for us to be there but both Andros and I got as much video footage as we could while we were in the area.

We arrived back at the hospital at about 4:30. I quickly got together as many medical supplies as I could pack in a large duffel bag I found. I also went back to the pharmacy and requisitioned several cases of formula and water, along with medication like antibiotics, antibiotic cream, bandage supplies and other medical supplies.

After I packed it all up, I phoned my friend Sonel and asked him to meet me in the front of the hospital to collect the things to take to Fondwa the next day. He came a few minutes later and I loaded them onto his cycle.

As I loaded my things into the van and then boarded, my heart was heavy and my mind was racing. How could we get help to her?

I had to find a way................

Note sent to Fondwa with Medical Supplies

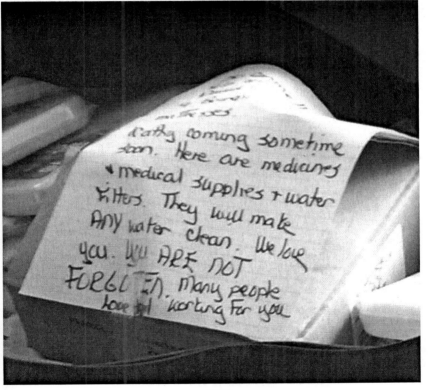

**Sr, Carmelle and Simone in Fondwa
January 21, 2010**

**Three
story
Fondwa
Guest
House
now in
ruins**

Chapter 17
The Last Day

Wednesday, January 26, was scheduled to be our last day of relief work. Our replacements were coming. They were scheduled to be there when we arrived back at the compound that evening. My goal that day was to make sure that all of the 12 patients under my care in the post op ward had all of their paperwork up to date. It was the most frustrating thing for me to try to figure out what was wrong with the kids when I first came. So if there was anything I could do to prevent someone else from having that frustration, I certainly wanted to take the necessary steps to make sure that happened.

I was able to give Peterson his new clothes and get him in the wheelchair and out of the room. I made sure that the one physical therapist got into our room to get evaluations done on all the kids in there, including Peterson.

Angelina, the girl with the gas gangrene who almost died, was doing well and, God be praised, by some miracle an aunt found her there. So she did have some family now with her. Her wounds were very bad and would take a long time to heal but at least we gave her a chance.

One of my other patients, Cronise, had the skin graft on her serious crush injury on her ankle the day before-- something that would never have happened in Haiti at any other time. She would probably do well and most likely heal completely in several months.

Stephenson, a 2 year old with a broken leg and an amputation on the other one, went back to surgery the day before and he was healing well. Adelor, a girl with two broken legs and a displaced hip had x-rays yesterday and things are looking good for her. Adaline, a 2 year old with a below-the-knee amputation was healing well, despite some early concerns for her infection.

I was to write in my blog later that evening:

> *I feel like I am leaving some children better off today than they were when I came here. I know my presence along with others allowed one child to live who likely would be dead today as I contemplate leaving.*
>
> *But then there are patients like Johanne, who sustained a closed head injury and has been in a coma since the earthquake with no real chance, barring a miracle, to recover and will not survive if she continues to   do as she is now. Her mom just won't give up hope so I have prayed with her each day.*
>
> *There is MUCH left to do. And there will need to be a commitment to the injured for many months to come. "*

What I was thinking was that there were less than 1000 doctors lived in Haiti. How they would take care of the hundreds of thousands of injured persons we were leaving behind? Most of them didn't care for the poor at all but for the very few patients who could pay for their private practice services. All I could think of was that there would need to be on-going relief teams coming regularly for at least a year until people could get back on their feet-some of them literally.

Also of great concern to me was the issue of prosthetics. There were virtually no prosthetics or rehab services available in Haiti. I knew of one NGO-Healing Hands for Haiti-an organization which assisted the disabled in Haiti. I had communicated with them several times in the past. But I also knew that their compound had been completely destroyed in the earthquake.

What would it be like for these people who were now not able bodied to try to maintain some semblance of life in this country where the able bodied struggle immensely just to survive? Tens of thousands were now the new amputee population in Haiti. One relief doctor we spoke with told me that he alone performed 350 amputations in the first three weeks.

I said my good-byes to Eddy who had been so valuable to me for the week. I was so grateful for him and his skill as a translator in assisting me. In addition his companionship was so comforting to me when I was feeling very isolated and alone.

As I was tying things up in my room about an hour before we had to go, a woman came in and spoke to me in Kreyol. I understood what she was saying asking me to come with her and followed her to the room next door as she instructed me.

In the room was a tiny baby, a few months old, in one of the cribs sleeping. She was in that room by herself. Just the woman-who turned out to be her grandmother-was there with her.

"We sa", she said in Haitian Kreyol as she pointed to the baby. "Look at this".

I made a comment about how beautiful the baby was but she kept speaking faster and faster-growing more and more animated and perhaps a bit agitated. I really was having trouble understanding what she was saying. Was something wrong with the baby? Did she want me to fix something?

A young Haitian girl came by who could speak some English and I asked her what the woman was saying. They spoke to each other for a few moments.

Then the young woman turned to me and said, "She said that this baby is hers now. Her daughter and all of her family were killed

211

in the earthquake and now she has the baby. She just doesn't know how she is going to take care of her by herself."

I understood now what the woman was trying to do. She wanted me to help her figure out how she was going to take care of this child when she could barely take care of herself. She might have thought I would take the baby and care for it myself. I found myself without words.

Of course, I had no answers to these kinds of questions of a similar nature that thousands upon thousands would be asking. Where are we going to live now that our house is destroyed? What are we going to eat now that our store is gone? How will our son finish school now that his school is a pile of rubble? Who will take care of the children who are without parents? Where will all of us live who now have no homes? Who will feed us and give us water? What will happen when the rains come?

How will we live NOW when we were barely surviving before all this happened?

This was the most helpless I had felt during the entire trip. I just looked at the woman. I had nothing to say to her. I tried to tell her that I wished I could help but all I could do was ask the Lord to send others her way who could help. I asked her if she wanted to pray. She said yes, half heartedly. I mustered up a prayer as best as I could. Turning around and leaving that woman there with the baby was one of the hardest things I had to do.

I just had no answers at all for her.

I was equally as concerned for the future as she was.

Even if I wasn't affected in the same way she was, because of all of the work I had done in Haiti I was very aware of the implications of this disaster on an already poverty ravaged nation. My heart was heavy as I walked back to my room, got

212

my backpack, and headed to the van for the last time. What a way to end.

I was quiet on the way home. I really didn't want to talk to anyone. Reality was beginning to take hold. I felt the shell cracking a bit, knowing the end was in sight.

Not all in disaster work is what you would hope it to be. I would write later in my blog that night to my closest friends:

> *"This has been a difficult week for me—not necessarily because of the disaster or what I have seen in the patients but what I have seen in some other's responses. I have seen many who are highly trained medical professionals who might do good work but lack a servant's heart. I have heard more complaints about the food, accommodations, riding conditions and other things relative to Haiti to last me a lifetime. For that reason it has been difficult for me. One day someone was actually complaining about the food we were given to eat and I responded to them, 'I am just grateful that I have something to eat today. At least your house didn't fall in on you'. It is that kind of thing that has worn on my psyche. More than I want to tell you."*

I had held these things inside, hoping they might have indicated extreme responses to the stress of the situation. I had withheld judgment as long as one could humanly do so. But I had reached my limit.

I heard those I was working with making fun of houses that had been destroyed and had a for sale sign out in front of it. I had heard someone on our team call the accommodations that a Dominican pastor's family had graciously given us "that pastor's nasty house" (even as I write it now I can hardly believe it) while in the same sentence state they hoped we wouldn't have to stay there on the way back. I had heard people make crude comments about the smell of decaying flesh. I had heard some of these same people criticize others for what they perceived as insensitivity to those who were injured.

Throughout the week, I had pushed these things aside and tried to continue my own work. I knew that my own personal and emotional attachment to the Haitian people before this disaster would temper any responses like this as a result of stress. But that was getting harder and harder to do with the degree of stress I was finding myself having to deal with.

Throughout the week, during these times of frustration with others who lacked sensitivity, I had sought refuge in two people that I had just met but who somehow seemed like they could be trusted. Both were missionaries-one worked at the compound and another was a missionary that worked with water filtration systems and was staying at the compound with us who shared a mutual friend with me who worked in the north. Both times I had asked them to pray that I would be patient and caring to people who "just didn't seem to get it."

One evening in particular I was struck with just what a servant's heart could be. I had met a woman in the bunk house who was in the next bunk to me. Her name was Connie. She was working with Samaritan's Purse. We spoke each evening in passing about how things had gone with us in our respective work.

One evening near the end of our time there, we were late getting back. We were the last of about 200 people to reach the food line. However, they didn't realize there were more people coming and all of the food had been given out. So when about 13 of us arrived we found ourselves waiting at the food serving window. The cooks and missionaries were surprised and went into overdrive to try to figure out what to do.

I happened to be the first person in the line of those who hadn't been served. So I just leaned back against the wall and waited.

They would work it out so I would just wait. Even if I didn't eat that night, with what I had experienced that week, who could complain?

I could see that the Spam cans were being opened and while I didn't relish the thought of some sort of canned meat product, I would be glad for whatever was put before me. We waited about 15 minutes and no one else who was eating made any attempt to move from their seats to do anything—that is except for Connie. I was just being introspective in the line waiting and listening to others in the line complain about what we might get or not get to eat, when she came up behind me.

She thrust a plate with a small piece of chicken and some beans and rice towards me and said "April, please let me share my dinner with you. I haven't touched any of this and I don't want to eat all of this with you standing here without any food."

I was so moved, I almost cried. I told her thank you but they were getting food for us and I would just wait.

She asked me again if I was sure because she really wanted to share with me. I almost accepted but I knew we would be getting food shortly and there was no reason for her not to eat her food. If we hadn't been getting food I would have been more likely to accept her offer to share. But since there was going to be food for us, I told her thanks again, that it was almost ready.

That, to me, was a real servant's heart. Not a single other person, including my own team members, did anything like that for me or anyone else in the line. I will never forget her generosity and thoughtfulness-although I am sure she would have to think hard to remember this situation in her own mind, if she did at all. It probably seemed pretty insignificant to her, but it was extraordinary to me. So extraordinary, that I went to great lengths with the Samaritan's Purse office to find her name and contact information when I returned home so that I could write her.

Our replacements had arrived that day. In our debriefing with them, we had a different slant on things after this week than those who had gone before us. We felt like things were more organized-at least an organized chaos now-and that there were some systems in place to provide safe and effective medical care with the hospitals where we were.

I concluded my blog entry that night with this:

> *"Thanks again for all of your support. Your support through God's grace has sustained me. And for that I am truly grateful. Nothing I have done this week has been on my own power. Even my work in Haiti as a whole has not been on my own power. It is only through the sustaining strength of the Lord that I am even here today. And as I am ever mindful of the blood of His son which was shed for my own sins, it is the least I can give back to help His children in Haiti."*

My last blog entry was written at 2:00 AM that night. I just couldn't sleep. There were so many things running through my mind. So many images, so many experiences, so many tragedies, some triumphs, so many heartbreaks, and some things I will likely never forget-even though I might wish I could. Even then, I had some insight as to what the next few weeks might hold for me.

> *" While I left here with a sense of hopelessness, not being able to fully grasp what it will take to fix this situation, I return knowing, that after seeing it firsthand, it can be fixed. But it will take tremendous effort on the international community and obedience of those followers of Jesus to help the Haitian people return to even a semblance of their life before January 12. January 12 will be the Haitians 9-11. That may help you*

get some sort of perspective. Entire sections of the city will need to be leveled- this includes many governmental buildings. The displaced will need to be placed again in some form of housing-to say nothing of the political and sociological implications. Many, many relatively small and moderate size ministries which sustain many people in Haiti will need to rebuild. As Sr. Carmelle said so poignantly this week- "twenty years of building was destroyed in about 1 minute." Those words are so true.

It will take millions of dollars of fund raising to do that in addition to what people have already given to large aid agencies for the immediate relief. I am worried about that. While our   organization has no formal buildings to replace, we are committed to about 22 people affiliated with Luke's Mission who are all currently displaced and we will need to support them finding safe and adequate housing and rebuilding their lives. Schools are all on hold. Praise God Romel finished in November or he would be delayed from beginning his practice next December. But our other medical student's school is delayed indefinitely and he has a complicated fracture of his leg   which will take months to heal.

It will take a lot to fix this problem. And while I remain skeptical because of past experiences with disasters there and ongoing aid, I do think it is possible. So I will just move forward as God directs me.

Since I began to work in Haiti I have always found the times of transitioning from this "first world" into that "third world"   difficult and vice versa. It would be so much easier I think for me to be in Haiti full time. But that isn't the Lord's plan for me now although it certainly has been my desire for a number of   years.

217

I find it hard to do things like use my MP3 player in Haiti or do other things that seem like home like play games or watch movies on the computer. And even after I get home, I find it takes several days to acclimate even now nearly 10 years after beginning to follow Jesus into Haiti. I look at people like Paul Farmer who lives in Haiti a lot of the time but also hob knobs with the rich and famous on the Haitian's behalf and practices medicine at Harvard. It seems hard for me to wrap my mind around how one does that so effortlessly like he seems to do it. Each time I leave Haiti, I find myself "ready to go home" but the conflict of that sense along with the knowledge that there are millions who do have that option make it hard for me.

But this time is different. It is usually hard for me to go home to fast food on each corner when I have just seen starving children or to use my sit down shower when there are those bathing in the street. I am very aware of those start contrasts when I return home.

But this time I will go home to work in a hospital with a level one trauma center when I have just come from a disaster with patients on every available floor space with IV's hanging from tree branches. I will go home to the finest neurosurgical options for patients with a closed head injury--when I have just left Johanne, a 7 year old who has a closed head injury and there is nothing they can do for her. She will die eventually in her coma with no options available to even see what is going on inside her tiny cranium.

I will go home to a first rate pediatric ward with every available medical technology there when I have left children who desperately need skin grafts for huge deep wounds who only option is my prayers that a plastic

218

surgeon will somehow come to Haiti and connect with them through some miracle.

This transition will be harder. Just sharing that with you will help. But I would ask for your prayers over these next few   weeks. I am leaving behind people I have come to love very   deeply not only for who they are but for the difference they have   made in my own life. I am deeply concerned about them in a   very different way this time. And keeping a foot in both worlds these next few months will be even more difficult."

The next day we traveled to the DR, then to the US, and home on Thursday.

Walls Guest House before the earthquake

Walls Guest House January 22, 2010 same view

Chapter 18
Transitions

I arrived home late on the evening of January28. Things began
to seem surreal almost immediately. I hadn't even gotten out of
the Miami airport before I got an email from two reporters-one
newspaper and one TV-wanting to meet me the next day or at
least at soon as possible. I was glad to be back onus soil and
knew that a hot shower and some food that seemed more familiar
to me awaited me soon.

Although, I wasn't anxious to see many people, I did feel a
compulsion to bring this story back home. So for that reason, I
wanted to try to see the reporters and talk to them while I could.
I spoke with both of them from the airport in Miami and set up
times to speak to them early the next morning. I insisted that
they come to the house. I didn't want to make any extra effort so
if they wanted to speak to me; I wanted them to come to me.
Both were happy to do that.

I sat down with the newspaper reporter in my living room and
talked to him for about an hour. The TV reporter came right as
the newspaper reporter finished. There perspective of what I
said was interesting for me to read:

> *"In her warm and cozy living room, April Perry sat on
> her cushy green couch, her greyhound Bailey
> nestled sleepily by her side, the dog's head in her lap.
> There were deep circles under Perry's warm, friendly
> eyes. Twelve hours or so earlier, she had been tending
> to children who were suffering from gangrene, hanging
> IVs from tree branches, changing dresses on grievous
> injuries, watching over those who had just had a leg or a*

foot amputated.

She had been in Haiti.

Despite all she had seen, despite all she had done, despite the psychological disconnect of returning to her comfortable northern Durham home, Perry said, "I went there feeling hopeless. But I've come back feeling hope." Just days after the devastating earthquake that has ravaged the island, Perry - a nurse at Duke University Medical Center and the founder and head of Luke's Mission, a Durham-based nonprofit that helps run medical missions and orphanages in Haiti - left on a disaster relief mission with the N.C. Baptist Men Relief Organization.

She spent 10 days on the Caribbean island, providing medical and post-operative care just outside the capital of Port-au-Prince. It was a facility - like all in Haiti now -overwhelmed by need, with insufficient supplies and personnel, and with a growing tent city outside its doors.

And yet.

"Amazingly to me, life is going on there, in Haiti," Perry said. "There are markets in the middle of the rubble. People are trying to living their lives. The city's not paralyzed. All the businesses are closed, but there are vendors out in the street and that gave me hope." Perry is no stranger to disaster. She has been to Haiti dozens of times and she spent six days helping out in New Orleans after Hurricane Katrina.

Consequently, "I wasn't shocked in Haiti," Perry said. "It wasn't worse that I could have imagined." she said. But still, she added, "it is terrible, just terrible."

221

For her, what was worst, she recalled, was seeing what had happened to the orphanage Luke's Mission had supported in the town of Fondwa, and the "two nuns I had grown to love" there.

The orphanage building had crumbled. The two nuns, with their 50 or so charges, were living outside, their walls pieces of clothing hung from trees.

"They had no water, no food, no sanitation," Perry said. "One of the nuns had a broken leg. And there was no help in sight."

Perry sighed deeply.

Despite her experience with disaster, despite her training, the extent of the effects of the earthquake, the endless numbers of children now orphaned, all those now with lost limbs, all that was emotionally draining and exhausting, Perry acknowledged.

"Still, I feel very, very good that we did what we needed to do," she said.

…On the morning after she returned from Haiti, Perry said she needed time to re-adjust from experiences like that. "I'm finding myself more in need of quiet time," she said. "Frankly, I'm really not anxious to see anybody."

But she knew she had to. "I had to bring this story back," Perry said. "Everyone has to know what has happened there, and how much help the Haitian people need."

In a follow up article, he added the information I gave him on what people could do that was the most helpful to the Haitians:

"April Perry has seen what Haiti needs. After 10 days on a medical mission in the earthquake-ravaged nation, Perry has seen the shortages of water and food and clothing and medical supplies. She understands that many here would want to send those items.

"But you have to consider what is best for the Haitian people," said Perry, a nurse at Duke Hospital and the founder and head of Luke's Mission, a Durham-based nonprofit that runs medical missions in Haiti.

"Do people want to do what is best for the Haitian people or do they want to make themselves feel better?"

In other words, she said, if you want to help and want to do more than just feel noble about it, "give money."

"That is, by far, the best thing people can do now. Collecting things, like clothing and supplies, will come, but right now, there's not enough infrastructure to get that stuff out to people."

In the best of times, she pointed out, "it's not easy to ship stuff to Haiti."

"Money works better now," she said.

Perry recalled her experiences in New Orleans, where she worked in disaster relief after Hurricane Katrina.

"There were trucks and trucks and trucks of clothes sent down to New Orleans after Katrina," she said. "It made people feel good -- but it was almost all wasted. We saw piles of clothes in a parking lot, all of it getting rained on. Everything was ruined because there was no way to get the clothing to people."

In a month or so, Perry said, collecting shoes and food would be a good idea because, then, she hoped, a distribution system would be in place. But in the meantime, "if you want to do something effective, help those who are doing the most good now."

She singled out two relief organizations, Samaritan's Purse and the American Red Cross, who were, she said, doing really good work.

"It might not make you feel as good," Perry said, "but sending money to organizations like that is absolutely the best thing you can do now."

Perry plans on returning to Haiti in two or three months. The nation's needs, she said, will still be there -- "particularly for medical care, that will remain an acute need."

When she returns, she said, her focus will be on the people affiliated with her organization, Luke's Mission. "We have to help them rebuild their lives," Perry said, "and we'll need help to do that."

I was able to take the next week off of work. Still feeling quite emotionally numb, I knew that the re-entry in this case would pose more conflicts than any time with a mission trip. I needed to have something in mind to say to those people who would ask in passing "Oh, how was Haiti?" At this time more than any, I needed to alter my expectations about how much people might or might not really care about what happened and what I saw there.

I decided to just say "It was the most intense experience of my life. Things are worse there than I probably can convey to you."

If they continued the conversation I could tell them more, but to be honest, most people didn't continue.

Having said that, I did a program for our church 4 days after I came back on a Wednesday night. It was good to be in a place where I knew people really cared and would listen and likely act as a result of receiving this information. It gave me a time to allow a bit of emotions to flow when I described the conditions there and what I did to try to help.

Drawing by Haitian patient of the earthquake

Chapter 19
The Great thanksgiving

Too many things seems took on new meanings of became symbolic to me those days immediately following my return as I began to thaw out emotionally from the intense experience of serving the Lord during the first response relief efforts following the Haiti earthquake.

The first Sunday after my return was our monthly communion Sunday. We have begun the tradition of taking communion through intinction-the process of moving to the front of the church, accepting the bread from our pastor and dipping it in the cup as our other pastor offers that and then returning to one's seat. While I always loved having the Lord 's Supper at the altar which had been the tradition prior, this particular day something very moving happened during the communion service.

We read our regular liturgy prior to the Lord's Supper. In the United Methodist Tradition this is called the Great Thanksgiving. Part of that is the prayer of confession and pardon.

Merciful God
We confess that we have not loved you with our whole heart.
We have failed to be an obedient church.
We have not done your will, we have broken your law, we have rebelled against your love, we have not loved our neighbors and we have not heard the cry of the needy. Forgive us we pray.
Free us for joyful obedience, through Jesus Christ our Lord. Amen.

I love that, at least monthly, we need to face the fact that we have neglected the poor and those in need around us. Although we should be mindful of it daily, at least it is something that we do corporately every 28 days or so each month. Those words meant so much more to me now as I have seen firsthand how the neglect of the country of Haiti by the international community and especially the US, has resulted in this terrible tragedy and its aftermath.

Don't get me wrong. There is nothing the average person person in Haiti did to deserve this nor is this some sort of celestial punishment from God for the "sins" of the country—if indeed there is such a thing.

On the other hand, we as average Americans may not be aware of the part that we have played in this tragedy. As members of a country which has, if not promoted the exploitation of Haiti, have done little to stop it, have played in this tragedy, we did play a part. I don't say that to induce guilt or any other feeling, but to make us aware.

No, the result of this natural disaster is due to neglect on the part of the international community in assisting the general populous in Haiti in overcoming a centuries old corrupt government, enabling non-accountability and a general self centeredness. To give you some perspective, in the 90's in the San Francisco area, an area with a population similar to that of the Port au Prince area had an earthquake which registered 7.0 as well. In that earthquake, 63 people died.

63.

Compare that with the 232,000 that are estimated to have died in Haiti 20 years later.

The reasons-from my perspective are twofold-lack of proper building codes and enforcements of those codes and lack of an infrastructure that would allow immediate first response efforts to maximize the number of injured who would survive their initial injuries from the earthquake.

So, yes, in many ways this is a result of poverty; but not poverty directly- poverty which has resulted from centuries of greed, conceit and lack of caring for the Haitian populous by both their own government and the international community.

So what does all that have to do with our communion Sunday?

As I was repenting of my sin of lack of caring of those in need corporately with my Christian community last Sunday, my heart was heavy. Yes, I had just spent 10 days working feverously to try to save lives and ease pain and suffering. It is easy to do that when there is a big event that draws the hearts and souls of most people.

But I am guilty of snapping at my office mate, neglecting the person with tears in their eyes who is clearly in pain but I have too much to do to stop and offer a kind word. I have avoided people in a public place because I just didn't have time to say hello, or allowed the phone to ring in the name of "screening my calls" just because I didn't feel like talking. Shoot, I even yelled one day at the Haitian nurses who weren't doing something the way I thought it should have been done.

I stayed at the altar just a bit longer at the nudging of the Holy Spirit asking for guidance and direction to try to be more like Jesus when these situations come up and praying for my beloved Haitian people that God would still look after then in this terrible tragedy.

As I returned to my seat, my mind was still focused on the confession. When I looked down and saw a piece of paper on the seat beside where I was sitting on top of my bible. I picked it up and it was a check, made out to our organization for earthquake relief. Someone in the line that was waiting their own turn to receive the Lord's Supper had left it there in my seat. I was moved to tears. As we each were being obedient to the calling of the Lord-mine to repentance, theirs to giving-He came to both of us through the sacrament of His body and blood. While I have never found intinction my preferred method of accepting the Lord's Supper, the moving to the front on this day seemed more symbolic than normal to me and the result, finding the check, seemed the same.

As we move forward towards repentance and ultimately obedience to the Lord's calling to serve the poor and needy in whatever way He calls us to, He will bring us to a more Christ-like place.

A friend recently asked me how it went in Haiti.

"You must be changed because of this" , she said.

Yes, I am changed—I hope that I am a more compassionate, giving, loving person who sees the needs of those around me more perceptively and, more importantly, can respond to those needs as they are revealed to me in the manner of Jesus Himself. I hope I am more reliant on the strength of the Lord because I surely can't do any of this on my own strength. I certainly didn't do it on my own strength in Haiti this time.

May all the glory go to the God of the Angel Armies, who in His infinite love for us, sent His only begotten Son to die in our place so that we could come to know His love and have the privilege that even the angels don't have-that of being redeemed.

May God help us help the people of Haiti overcome their own leader's sins of greed and corruption.

Chapter 20
"It is not me but Christ who lives in me…"

The email came as a great surprise.

I was doing some final work before calling it a day and noticed at 9:00 PM a prompt that I had a new email on my work account. When I checked it I noticed that it was from Ron, the physician in my previous job who I had worked with.

Ron and I had what I would call a good relationship… considering. He was superb physician who took care of children who had congenital heart disorders, specializing in those who had heart rhythm problems. There are few in the country that had the uncanny skills that he has at identifying the exact place in the heart where the abnormal heart rhythm originates so that it can be electrically removed-a procedure known as a radio frequency ablation-restoring hopefully the normal heart rhythms for the child. He spent many 20 hour days in the cardiac catheterization lab trying to locate the microscopic location of the problem. There are many children out there today walking around living normal lives because of his skills and commitment to their care.

Ron was known as being temperamental. Many would say that is an understatement. He was emotionally boisterous, often speaking his mind with little filtering and possessed little, if any, tact. However, for those patients and families he interacted with, he was the model of compassion and professionalism. He had a history of going through clinician assistants rather quickly, all of whom found him to difficult to work with. Additionally, he often found himself in hot water with the administration of the pediatric cardiology department for which he worked related to his interpersonal interactions.

I had taken a job in 1996 to start up the Pediatric Cardiology clinical research program. I had managed that program for about 4 years and it was now running quite nicely. I yearned for more patient contact and less administrative work. So when the physician extender clinician position came open to work with him, I knew what I might be in for as I chose to apply for it.

I worked with Ron for 7 more years. Despite the fact that we were on opposite sides of the Duke-Carolina men's basketball rivalry, and he took every opportunity to needle me about that when UNC was were on a losing streak or lost to Duke, we had a good working relationship for the most part. His antics didn't bother me as much as they had previous people and I brought to the job a level of clinical expertise that he had not had in a clinician before. He quickly became aware of the real value that a skilled clinician could have in helping to manage the outpatient practice as we developed our working relationship the first year.
I really enjoyed the clinical work with these kids and their parents. I got to do a lot of teaching and working directly with them on modifying their lives to live with the disease and Ron came to rely on me for that part of the clinical care.

Ron knew that I was a Christian. He was Jewish. Although he didn't attend synagogue regularly, he always celebrated the high holy days. He considered being Jewish something that was part of who he was as a person. Our clinical practice was closed on Rosh Shoshanna and Yom Kippur.

In private conversations with me, he was never shy about pointing out the hypocrisies that seem to pervade the Christian world and I was never far from his skeptical eye with regards to how I lived my life. He didn't have much time for "that Messiah thing" as he referred to it, but even though I was often the brunt of his skepticism about how Christians lived their lives out around him, I knew he respected me for my beliefs.

He loved that fact that I was involved in Haiti. After each trip he would want to know what happened and I would detail the kinds of patients I saw there. More than once, I asked him to go with us and I think he really want to but just couldn't muster up the courage to do it. He said he felt that he wouldn't be useful there and wouldn't really be able to do very much to help. Despite my attempts to convince him that his skills would be invaluable there, I wasn't able to get him on the ground in Haiti.

Even though he was Jewish, Ron always gave me a Christmas present. It was my practice not to give presents to my supervisors. I just never really felt comfortable with that. But he always bought something for me. And it wasn't just some silly gift. They were always things that showed that he had actually thought about me when purchasing the gifts-things like a UNC basketball rug, or a beautiful copper sculpture. Not mass produced things but thoughtful things.

In 2005, Haiti went through a very difficult time. They actually made the headlines in most US papers for several weeks. A coup had occurred the year before and rebels had forces the current president, Aristide, to leave the country under the cover of darkness. What happened subsequently was a period of severe political instability, with little governmental services available. The UN had come in to take over the country until an election could occur. It was a very dark time for our work in Haiti. Several people we knew were murdered by gangs which roamed the streets undeterred.

So it had been a hard year for me with respect to my work in Haiti. That year, he brought the Christmas present in to me on the day I was leaving for my Christmas break. It wasn't wrapped in the fancy way previous ones had been wrapped. He paid people to wrap them-and they were beautiful. It just was an envelope. I opened the envelope and in it was a check for Luke's Mission for a considerable amount of money. He told me that he had thought about it and that for this particular year he thought that nothing would mean any more to me than to have some financial support for the work in Haiti that meant so much to me.

To say I was overcome with emotion would have been an understatement. I told him that he was right and thanked him profusely for doing this. It began a practice that he has continued to this day. The next year he told me he wanted to give donations to all of the people he gave presents to, instead of purchasing gifts for them and asked for my help in finding some good organizations who did effective work with children across the world to give to in honor of those he wanted to give presents to. I was thrilled when I got my donation to UNICEF from him for that Christmas.

After I left to take another job, we kept in touch once or twice a year just general greetings or when I would need some clinical advice from him about something.

So, that night, when this email came in with nothing written on the subject line, I just assumed it was something unrelated to Haiti.

I wasn't prepared for what I read:
> *"April,*
>
> *I just had to take a second and tell you how proud everyone here is of you. I know you do what you do for the right reasons, and accolades don't mean much to you, but I think some of us live our lives of "high character" vicariously through people like you.*
>
> *Ron"*

It is hard to describe the feeling I felt when I read that. I wasn't really sure what he meant by "lives of high character", but I hope he was referring to the effect that the love of Christ has had in my life and how he might have perceived it being acted out—at least that is what I hope. I hoped what he was referring to was the reflection of the character of Christ that he had seen in the way my life was lived.

I prayed and asked the Lord how to respond so that I could use this opportunity to continue the witness to the impact His Holy Spirit had had in my life and convey that to him. Almost immediately the words of Paul came to mind and so my response was formed around them.

> *"Ron:*
>
> *I am deeply touched by your words below. More than I can say...*
> *I do this not on my own strength, power or desire---"It is no longer I who live, **but Christ who lives in me**"* *Galatians 2:19.*
> *Thanks*
>
> *April"*

I had been part of the process of reflecting the love of Christ to Ron and others in that department. I was grateful it seemed that His efforts had been fruitful. It was one more example of how this work in Haiti has provided me with such rich opportunities to witness to the power that Christ can have in a person's life.

Chapter 21
Haiti February, 2010

This article describes the situation in Haiti several weeks after the earthquake.

"Even in normal times, Edwin Andre has all he can do to eke out a living from the corn, tomatoes and sweet potatoes he coaxes from an acre plot in northern Haiti. His wife, Roselaine Cius, peddles the produce roadside and cooks rice-and-bean plates from a stick-frame lunch shack to help support their family of eight. Suddenly, though, eight hungry mouths soared to 18 after siblings and in-laws from earthquake-ravaged Port-au-Prince fled by rattletrap bus to this sweep of farmland, a two-hour drive from the capital. The couple's spare, concrete house -- no bigger than an average one-bedroom apartment in the United States -- is packed to bursting.

Food once converted to cash goes to feed the homeless loved ones. Money is now so short that the pair doubt they will be able to buy seeds for the crucial spring planting season that is only weeks away.

"I don't see how we will have enough money," said Cius, 40, sweating under a porkpie hat as she ladled rice from a charcoal-heated pot. "There's no way. There's no money."

The effects of the Jan. 12 earthquake that flattened much of Port-au-Prince are rippling powerfully across rural Haiti, the poorest swath of the poorest nation in the Western Hemisphere. Villagers are near the breaking point as they try to accommodate tens of thousands of displaced city dwellers just when they would be putting their precious resources into preparing for planting. In desperation, some have resorted to eating their meager seed stocks or killing their chickens and goats to feed the influx, rather than keeping them to sell.

Fertilizer is expensive and seeds for cereal crops are in short supply because of damage to the seaport in the capital and wary buying by wholesalers. Farming areas southwest of Port-au-Prince were also devastated by the 7.0 quake, which ruined whole towns, such as Leogane, near the epicenter, and damaged vital irrigation channels.

Agricultural officials and aid workers worry that while global efforts to help quake victims in Port-au-Prince are hitting their stride, the ripple effect in the countryside threatens to stymie some farming and worsen conditions in areas where most people already scrape by on less than $2 a day. Some experts warn of a quiet agricultural disaster in the making.

Relief workers say only a tiny portion of international aid has been earmarked for rural Haitians, who account for most of the country's 9 million people. Of $23 million sought for farmers as part of an urgent appeal by the United Nations, donor governments have provided only about $2 million for agriculture.

"These communities were already the poorest part of the country. The countryside is extremely poor and they have very few means to cope," said Alexander L. Jones, Haiti emergency-response manager for the U.N. Food and Agriculture Organization. "It is putting a lot of stress on families."

Jones said spot surveys show that the average size of rural families has nearly doubled, from five members to nine. Agencies are scrambling to import 2 tons of seeds, plus hoes, shovels and wheelbarrows, for the farmers, many of whom lost their hand tools under collapsed homes near Port-au-Prince. The first shipment of 15,000 implements arrived last week. Relief workers are also turning to the Dominican Republic next door to hunt for seed varieties that are also planted in Haiti.

"The planting season is approaching. We've got to deliver these seeds before it starts," said Roberto Borlini, who works for an Italian nonprofit called GVC that plans to distribute seeds and tools to 2,000 families near Petit-Goave, hard-hit town southwest of the capital. GVC and at least a couple of dozen other foreign aid agencies, including such major players as CARE, have focused part of their efforts on rural areas. But farmland assistance has been overshadowed by the critical needs in Port-au-Prince.

Haiti's agricultural sector was a basket case even before the quake. Years of deforestation have denuded much of the countryside, helping to degrade overworked soil that doesn't hold nutrients well and yields food reluctantly. In a country that grows rice and corn, Haitians get most of their cereals and many other goods from abroad, making them extraordinarily expensive. A chicken can cost $7.

Tropical storms two years ago caused $200 million in damage to food crops. Since the earthquake, the nation's agriculture minister, Joanas Gue, has called on creditor nations to help by forgiving Haitian debt. In many ways, relief workers say, it's fortunate that so many of the displaced found shelter with relatives. The arrangement provides a smoother way to deliver aid and offers the homeless a healthier alternative to sleeping in the encampments that have popped up in Port-au-Prince. But the exodus of an estimated 480,000 people from the capital has flooded dirt-road villages with city folk who need to eat and have little interest in hoe-and-spade work. Anyway, there were already too few farm jobs to go around.

"I don't go out. I don't hear music. I don't see the things I'm used to seeing," said bored-looking city dweller Richemononde Cius, 27, the sister of Roselaine. She and other family members piled into a bus headed for the country two days after the earthquake, which split the family house in Port-au-Prince, killing a cousin. As a child, Richemononde Cius spent summers with her farming relatives, but she never wanted to live in the country. She now bides her time waiting for ideas from her fiancé in Boston on how to join him there.

The 10 newcomers pitch in as they can, then stay outside in the dirt yard as late as possible before bunking down on concrete floors covered wall to wall with people. Roselaine Cius said that feeding the arrivals -- they call themselves "deportees" -- means she has less food to turn into plates of rice, beans and bits of chicken to sell for $1.75 at her tin-roof hut. Most of her customers are in the same boat, though, with fewer able to buy.

"Every morning I have to think about where to get food for all these people," said her 53-year-old husband. "I can't let them go hungry."

With funds dwindling, he and his wife have yet to buy seed for the spring crop of beans, maize and rice. Half a mile up the road, Luckner Monrinvil and his family have taken in 10 relatives from Port-au-Prince in two weather-beaten shanties. The difficulty of finding something to eat has brought constant anxiety. A few spoonfuls of rice or a bit of boiled breadfruit, fortified with pieces of processed fish, may be all anyone gets.

The recent harvest of peppers and sweet potatoes was a flop, a fact Monrinvil attributes to the earth's trembling. He has no cash for seeds. Monrinvil, 53 years old but taut as a teenager, offers to show a visitor his half-acre field, a hike of a mile or so. Under a scorching afternoon sun, he sets out past verdant stands of corn and a wide irrigation channel that also serves as a swimming pool and bathtub for residents. But about halfway, Monrinvil reconsiders and asks to turn back. He is feeling the first pangs of hunger, and they remind him that he lacks a plan for food this day.

238

There are so many mouths to feed." [Ken Ellingwood Los Angeles Times, February 23, 2010]

**Building destroyed Port au Prince Haiti
January, 2010**

Chapter 22
November 2010

As I put the final touches on this book, having re-read it several times, I see how prophetic many of my thoughts and concerns were—all of which were written nearly 9 months ago.

It is now 10 months after the earthquake. I wrote nearly this entire book within the first three weeks of my return.

However, today, 1,500,000 people still remain homeless and in sheet shanties or tents shelters as a result of losing their home on January12, 2010.

The Median Strip tents in Carrefour are still standing and have expanded. In the last few months several children have been killed as traffic has increased and families continue to live on the median strip.

In May, 2010, aide agencies were asked by the Haitian government o stop food distribution because it was "competing with the local economy". What they didn't say is that those who were standing in the food lines wouldn't have the resources to purchase food from local markets anyway. So, yet again in Haiti, the have's will continue on and the have not's will struggle daily.

In September, I took a team of 18 people to Haiti to do medical clinics there. We slept in tents for the whole week because the guest house had been destroyed and wasn't rebuilt yet.
In the weeks after the earthquake, first world medical care continued to be available to the Haitians that needed it. Many hospitals in the US and other first world countries sent personnel and equipment down to assist with health care provision.

However, because many of them didn't understand completely what was involved in providing care in a country so depleted of resources like Haiti, many problems were caused as they tried to practice high tech medicine in the third world. These problems were the basis of many an ethics conference for the workers upon their return to the facility where they practiced.

One of the biggest surprises to me was the way the international prosthetic community stepped up and provided prosthetics for the tens of thousands of new amputees. These people would have had no chance of a productive life in pre earthquake Haiti with an amputation. Low tech prosthetics were made right in Haiti and the Haitians were taught how to make them to provide a small boost to the economy. Not everyone who needed one was able to get one immediately but I remain very hopeful that the prosthetic community will continue to support Haiti for years to come.

A cholera epidemic has broken out effecting, in the last 39 days, over 20,000 people at the time of this writing, with nearly 1500 people dead. Tens of thousands more are expected to be ill or dead before it is anticipated the outbreak will be under control.

The government remains as impotent as it was before the earthquake. Large aid organizations are getting more and more frustrated as they try to work within the governmental structure. Just last week, Franklin Graham from Samaritans Purse was on network television expressing his frustration at the Haitian government withholding IV solutions they needed for the treatment of cholera victims.
Elections took place last week, November 28, 2010. The results are not in but only 3.5% of the population actually cast a vote.

The international community is outraged at the lack of money that has been spent on the rebuilding of Haiti. Billions were donated from all over the world but many of the larger aid organization have only spent a fraction of what was donated.

The reasons for this remain unclean. This is an entry from my blog in May, 2010 which still reflects the situation now 7 months later (November, 2010)

~~~~~~~~~~~~~~~~~~~~~~~~~~~~~~~~

Where is the rest of the $685 million given for Haiti relief?
In a recent news report, CBS followed the money from 4 large aid organizations donated to assist in the relief efforts following the Haitian earthquake. We are now 4 months post event. Tens of thousands are living in shelters made only of tarps suspended on wooden poles. I have personally seen pictures and video of rains and how they affect this type of housing structure. I have seen small rivers running through these refugee compounds and people living under plastic that we would use to wrap a new couch in.

Yet the Red Cross has received $444 million dollars. Care has received $24 million, Catholic Relief $165 million and the Clinton Bush foundation $52 million for a total of $685 million dollars for t he relief efforts. How much has been spent now 4 months later? $135.75 million. Less than 1/5 of what has come in to these large organizations.

Even allowing for the fact that it is reasonable to hold back some money for longer term efforts over time, the enormity of the suffering that continues each minute of the day in Haiti requires these organizations to do more than what they have done to bring relief to the Haitians. Relief should have been accomplished in the first 8 weeks at the most. Stable and safe housing, sanitation, access to food and water and clothing are the immediate needs addressed by disaster relief. Yet over 200,000 people still remain displaced in horrific conditions, making their way each day as they can. The refugee camps are reported to be unsafe with women especially being brutalized and exploited. Stealing is common. Sanitation is virtually nonexistent. The first case of diphtheria occurred in one of the camps just this week. More is likely to come later.

Why are we not holding these organizations accountable for the use of the money that was given to provide immediate relief to the Haitian and to appease their suffering? 80% of the funds remain unspent, now 4 months post earthquake. 80% of the money we gave to help these people.

It is commonly accepted that the Haitian government can make red tape bureaucracy of this country look like a walk in the park. However, even with the difficulties that exist in working directly with the government, the large aid organizations could restructure their funding to allow smaller non profits with more grass root contacts to apply for grants for housing projects, transitional and permanent. Other supplies like beds, latrines and household water filtration systems are easily distributed. But no plan exists that anyone is aware of to begin this.

The Haitians have suffered much in their lives. Many call them resilient. And that would be appropriate. However, giving up isn't an option unless they want to end up dead.

The lazy in Haiti don't survive.

To see children walking in waist deep water through a shanty town made up of tarp structures that are nearly falling down is more that heartbreaking. It is inhuman and should not be tolerated.

I return to Haiti next week for the first time since my own first response relief work in January. Our organization has spent about 45% of the money designated for relief efforts to date. I am returning as part of the accountability structure of our organization to meet with people and talk with them in person about how the situation is for them and how they have used the funds we have designated for their food, water, shelter and other necessities.

We need to hold the aid agencies accountable for their lack of providing immediate relief now 4 months later. And lend support to the smaller non profits that stabilize Haiti on a good day before the earthquake and are now the mainstay of the day to day work to just help the Haitians survive until tomorrow.

Tent City built in the road median
Carrefour, Haiti
June, 2010

Epilogue

So much happened so quickly upon my return from Haiti. Having assessed as well as I could the impact of the earthquake on those affiliated with Luke's Mission, we felt we needed to take immediate action to see that they were cared for as much as possible.

While I was in Haiti, donations came in for earthquake relief to our organization in records amounts. We were able to supply monthly stipends for a number of families associated with our ministry to see that they had food and water until we could see how the government might try to stabilize the situation later in the year.

We also ramped up our water filtration program purchasing as many water filters and getting them to Haiti as the money came in. Sawyers, our distributor, found that they were so successful they opened a plant right in Port au Prince making it easier to obtain them once funds were procured.

People were generous beyond belief. We received contributions from people we didn't know. It was a blessing to have resources to be able to help those affiliated with our ministry. Some of the undertaking we were able to do as a result of these donations are listed below.

$100 monthly stipends from March until September for 7 families affiliated with our ministry to help provide food and clean water during the crisis until they could get back on their feet.

Rebuilding of the bath house for Mission of Hope, our partner for the Haiti Mission team to assist them in getting their facilities ready to receive teams again.

Rebuilding of the security wall, external walls and roof for the home of Jules Remy and family, translator for Luke's Mission

Purchase of 30 stacking Nap cots to use as temporary beds for the children in the Mission of Hope and Fondwa Orphanages until permanent beds and facilities can be replaced

Purchase of 50 beds to be used in Fondwa

Purchase of 150 water filters from Sawyers water filters during their buy one get one free earthquake relief sale which were distributed to people in Cite Soleil immediately after the earthquake

Salary for Emmanuel Occidor, Luke's Mission employee to help distribute the funds, oversee the construction and the water filters. This money will provide income for him to help support his family.

Building 4 transitional shelters for the Fondwa nuns and orphans Purchase of 24 nap cots for Hands and Feet project as they start a new orphanage to help them assist with the post earthquake orphans

Provision of startup pharmacy for Sr. Carmelle for the new Container clinic in Fondwa.

Over the next months, I was asked to speak countless times at churches, civic organization and other public venues to help continue to bring the story of the Haitian earthquake to the people in my sphere of influence. I prayed each time that God would get the message across to this group of people that He intended through my words.

Update: Johanne, March, 2010
Imagine my surprise when I received the following blog entry from St. Damien's Hospital early in March, 2010. It was titled

appropriately *"Resurrection"*. The portion of the blog entry on Johanne is copied below:

> *"Gena and colleagues [at St. Damien's] have been working tirelessly to get many Haitians "back on their feet" and the following is just one story of inspiration from Gena.*
>
> *When we first met Johanne we were really worried about her. She had a severe brain injury that left her as good as dead as far as many were concerned. The doctors assured us there was little hope of a resurrection. Some weeks ago I wrote about Johanne and I remember writing that we are people of hope and we would continue to hope for her. Her faithful mother and grandmother never left her side. Norma and her*

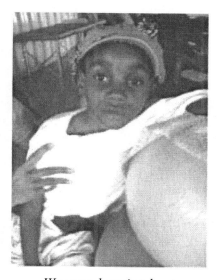

> *team of therapists were always working with Joanne and other mothers in the hospital were all wishing for.*
>
> *Joanne to wake up, for her to get out of "her tomb!" Three months have almost gone by and how is Joanne now?*
>
> *...Johanne is so much better! She is now very responsive but when we were taking the photo she just wanted to sleep.*
>
> *We were begging her to open her eyes for the photo and she gave that little sheepish smile before consenting to our plea. She is, by the way, modeling one of my NEW three new caps! You will notice Norma is also*

247

*wearing a new cap so you can see what a
trendsetter I am. Do you see how Johanne looks like her
Mam? This Mam deserves any number of awards
for unfailing courage,   strength, hope and love.*

*We are very happy with the progress Johanne has made.
If you   ask her to give you her hand she will try and lift
her hand to you and it is obvious that she is aware of
what is going on around her. She no longer needs a
feeding tube and while she is very thin we are hopeful
that she will continue to regain weight. She is now able
to complain when she is not comfortable and she makes
noises when she wants to communicate. She smiles;
Oh the beauty of a smile from Johanne!*

*Johanne is a beacon of hope for all of us. She suffered so
much, lost so much, could so easily have died. But
she is a fighter. She, like the Haitian people, is not going
to give up without a fight and luckily for her she has a
host of people around her to help her fight. To me this is
the story of the day! All the people that love*

*Johanne
are with
her every
day,
helping
her shake
off the
forces of
darkness
that want
to claim
her for*

*death and for coma. All she needed was this love to help
her fight and with this love she is doing great work
herself! She has a long way to go but the important thing*

248

is that through our program she will have very good
care and she will be given every opportunity to improve!

I was shocked to read of Johanne's recovery. She wasn't out of the woods by a long ways but I would never have expected to see her respond to anything much less make meaningful responses.

Update: Peterson, May 2010

Eddy was able to locate Peterson for me so I could see him when I returned to Haiti in May 2010. It was the first time I had been back since the earthquake relief work. Since medical records are not kept on a regular basis, it took quite some work for him to be able to find him.

We made arrangements to meet his mother-yes, his mother-at a n area of the city near where they lived and she would take us to their home.

When we arrived at the meeting place, she was there waiting for her. The adventure of the trek to their home would be a chapter in this book. But, suffice it to say, we walked through many back streets of a slum area for about 30 minutes, following her to the place where they lived-a small shack literally on top of a landfill.

I recognized Peterson immediately and from the smile on his face, it was clear he recognized me too. We sat down with the family who was there and his mother, a beautiful young Haitian woman told me the story.

On the day of the earthquake, she had dropped Peterson off at his aunts and taken his older brother to school. His brother had been killed at his school when the earthquake occurred. She had looked for Peterson for over two weeks. She went to every hospital until she finally arrived at St. Damien's the day after I had left to return home. Peterson wasn't an orphan but had a family that was looking for him and did find him. She told me that he had told her about the white woman who had helped him get a new tee shirt and the wheelchair. She was able to take him home. He was given an appointment for one of the first prosthetics that St. Damien's did for the children that they treated. He had his prosthetic there and put it on for me. He could walk very normally with it. The shoe was even matching his other shoe. It slipped right over his stump. It was fitted to allow him a bit of room to grow but she would need to take him back as he grew to get replacements.

His mother was a delightful woman. One of my favorite pictures was of Peterson and Angelina in their wheelchairs on the day I left. For many months I had that as the desktop photo on my Blackberry. I showed him the picture on my phone so he would know that I had not forgot him either.

It was a wonderful reunion. I feel sure that Peterson will manage to continue to heal. The most important thing is that he was reunited with his family. It was a wonderful experience to be able to see him again.

Peterson Louis with his prosthesis, June, 2010

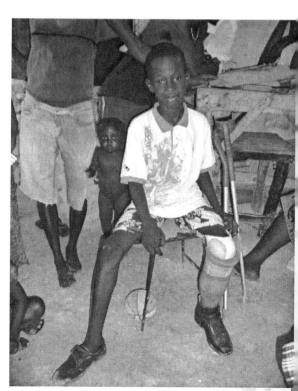

April,, Peterson and Madame Louis, June 2010

Update: Fondwa, May 2010

We kept up with Sr. Carmelle throughout the following few months. Trying to help them was a priority for us but as they are located in such a remote area, it was even more difficult. We sent her money to assist with the children's care, 50 beds for them to sleep in, water filters and other necessities. Several other agencies including the Canadian military finally came to help them about 6 weeks after the earthquake. The local peasants built a temporary shelter where the 64 orphans-12 more than when I was here in January- and the nuns were all living.

We visited in May, 2010. This shelter which held the 64 orphans, was a shoddily made tin shelter held up by small trees used as poles throughout the structure. It had no windows or lights and a mud floor. Some children had beds but others were sleeping on the mud floor on mattresses. The whole two days we were there it poured down rain. We just didn't find this situation acceptable on any level-for Haiti or anywhere else in the world. In fact, it was the worst thing I had seen since the earthquake happened.

We were deeply concerned with this situation. As you can imagine, these living quarters posed a very serious health risk for these children and the nuns who were living in this shelter. Disease breeds in dark, warm and wet environments-everything this shelter was. Disposing of trash and human/animal waste remained a problem there. We saw both human and animal waste along the walking paths to the place where we stayed while there. One child coming down with typhoid, TB or dysentery, could have presented the community with an unprecedented outbreak which could have endangered the health and lives of all of the children. The possibility of an outbreak in which many or all of the children getting seriously ill or dying was a very real one-one which would occur in Haiti later when the cholera epidemic occurred.

Fondwa shelter housing 65 children and 14 nuns

Inside Fondwa Shelter-orphans sleeping on the dirt and mud

Upon seeing the situation there, the board members of Luke's Mission immediately agreed that it needed to be remedied quickly. While all the groups there are concerned with this situation, many are working on many different fronts with the Haitian earthquake relief efforts. We saw this as an immediate priority and had to take action to do what we can to correct it and correct it quickly.

We met with Father Joseph Phillipe and Sr. Carmelle Voltaire, the community leaders, on Saturday May 29 while we were in Fondwa. Per Father Joseph there is no specific plan for constructing transitional shelters for the children or sisters proposed by any other sponsoring organization currently. After speaking with him about the potential health risks he agreed with us that the immediate need was to provide clean and safe living structures for the orphans and nuns and that this should take precedent over all other work there at this point. However, he indicated that they had no funds with which to do this. He was unaware of any funding from any of the other sponsoring organizations designated for transitional shelters for the nuns and orphans.

Seeing the seriousness of the need and knowing the public health implications for this situation for the orphans and their nun caretakers, Luke's Mission, proffered a plan to Joseph and Sr. Carmelle, that morning which would include the building of 5 transitional shelters-2 larger shelters to house the orphans and 2 smaller ones to house the 9 nuns. These were similar to the shelters which are currently there and were constructed by the Canadian military and others after the earthquake. These shelters would be made of wood, be safer in the event of another earthquake as well and will be able to be used for many purposes when a permanent orphanage is underwritten and built in the future. Father Joseph showed us a small parcel of land next to some of the other shelters which the peasant association owns and felt the transition shelters could be built there. Because of the urgency of the situation, we were in need of raising funds for this project quickly. Each day that passed where the children and nuns were living in these conditions, added to the risk they will contract a serious disease. The reality was that the current living situation is a public health nightmare. Only God's grace and care had prevented something from occurring there already.
We needed $25,000 to build these shelters-$7500 for each of the larger shelters and $5000 for the two shelters for the nuns. Local Haitian labor would be used to assist skilled local workers in obtaining salaries while working on this project with oversight of knowledgeable construction persons so that the new buildings will be assured of being structurally sound.

We were very fortunate that our ministry partner, Hands and Feet project, immediately came to our aid with enough money to get the nuns and children into a dry and clean shelter. Emmanuel oversaw the construction and we had them in new shelters within 5 weeks form the time we visited and saw the horrific conditions in which they were living.

Fondwa will take years to rebuild. Sr. Carmelle and Simone are struggling under the stress of the situation. We continue to support them as we can. Sr. Carmelle is looking forward to starting a new orphanage in an area adjacent to Fondwa where there are many children who need care.

Pictures of the shelters they were living in when we arrived in May, 2010 and the new ones we built for them are on our website-www.lukesmission.com.

Another organization donated a refurbished shipping container which had been made into a clinic to Fondwa. We were able to provide her with a year's worth of medication to start up her clinic.

New Fondwa Shelters for orphans and nuns, June 2010

1.5 million people are still living like this a full year after the earthquake. Photos by April Perry

256